Computer Processing of Social Science Data Using OSIRIS IV

Judith Rattenbury
Paula Pelletier
Laura Klem

Computer Processing of Social Science Data Using OSIRIS IV

Judith Rattenbury
Paula Pelletier
Laura Klem

Survey Research Center
Institute for Social Research
The University of Michigan

1984

Library of Congress Cataloging in Publication Data:
Rattenbury, Judith.
    Computer processing of social science data using
OSIRIS IV.

    Bibliography: p.
    1. OSIRIS (Electronic computer system)   2. Social
sciences--Computer programs.   I. Pelletier, Paula.
II. Klem, Laura.   III. Title.
H61.3.R38   1984   001.64'25   84-2727
ISBN 0-87944-295-6 (pbk.)

ISR Code Number 4652

Published 1984 by:
Institute for Social Research,
The University of Michigan, Ann Arbor, Michigan

6 5 4 3 2 1
Manufactured in the United States of America

TABLE OF CONTENTS

v

List of Figures

PREFACE

Since our earlier ISR volume, *Data Processing in the Social Sciences with OSIRIS*, was published in 1974 there have been significant changes in the computer programs available for management and analysis of social science data. The present volume was undertaken in order to bring the material up to date.

While the purpose and organization of this volume remain similar to that of the earlier book, technical changes in computer processing have resulted in substantial changes in the text. In the present volume the use of disk for data storage and computer terminals for interactive data processing is emphasized, the most recent version of OSIRIS is used for examples, and a chapter is devoted to processing hierarchically structured data.

Laura Klem, who has been responsible for revising the original work, appears as co-author of the volume. We are grateful to Frank Andrews, who first suggested a new volume and who has supported the project through several drafts. Marita Servais and Greg Duncan read a draft of the entire manuscript and provided comments and suggestions that resulted in important improvements. Tina Bixby and Maryellen McSweeney provided helpful comments on portions of the manuscript. The particularly demanding wordprocessing was performed by Rhonda McDougal, Pamela Melton, and Katherine Metcalf.

This monograph is intended to guide researchers in the field of social science (or their assistants) through all the stages necessary for processing data with a computer. No previous knowledge of computers is assumed, although it is expected that readers will have at least theoretical knowledge of data collection and analysis.

It is hardly ever necessary these days for people to write their own computer program in order to use the computer to process their data. Instead, packaged general-purpose programs, already written by computer professionals, are available to the computer user at most installations. All the prospective user of the computer has to do (assuming that a few basic principles are understood) is to find the name of the program which performs what is required, and prepare a few control statements according to the writeup for the program. A number of such packaged programs are used in this monograph as examples of how a particular task can be achieved with the computer. Most of these programs are from the OSIRIS package, along with a few of the general-purpose utilities provided by IBM for its 360 computer. OSIRIS is a package of about 50 programs for the management and analysis of social science data, jointly developed by the component centers of the Institute for Social Research using funds from the National Science Foundation, the Inter-University Consortium for Political Research and other sources. OSIRIS is currently available at approximately 200 other installations in the USA and abroad. Even if OSIRIS is not available at a particular installation, the general principles and processes described are still relevant and can be achieved by other programs.

Data processing problems multiply as the amount of data increases. Thus, some of the steps and procedures described here may be unnecessary for small bodies of data. The strategies are geared to a typical study at the Survey Research Center which might involve data from a survey in which about 1500 respondents are each asked about 500 questions.

The monograph is divided into eight chapters. Chapter 1 introduces the basic components of computers and the different kinds of software necessary for using a computer. Chapter 2 discusses types of data and some of the preliminary data collection phases prior to computer processing. Chapters 3-6 go step by step through the data processing stages which must be accomplished before analysis can be undertaken. Chapter 7 outlines different kinds of analysis and treats two frequently used OSIRIS analysis programs in detail. Chapter 8 describes the kinds of errors commonly made when using a computer for data processing, and gives some hints on how to avoid them. Sample setups and computer output for all the major data processing steps can be found in the appendices.

This monograph is not a reference manual for using OSIRIS programs. For a complete description on all aspects of the OSIRIS III package, reference should be made to the OSIRIS III Manual, Vols. 1-6 ([1]).

We are grateful to Laura Klem for many helpful suggestions and criticisms; to Avram Cohen, Carolyn Geda, Susan Marshall and Richard Warren for their useful comments; to Ellen Bronson and Mary McCleer who shared the burden of preparing various drafts, and to Ellen Bronson who typed the final manuscript.

Paula Pelletier
Computer Services Facility

Judith Rattenbury
Survey Research Center

January 1974

Chapter 1

INTRODUCTION TO COMPUTER HARDWARE, SOFTWARE, AND CONTROL LANGUAGES

1.1   Use of Computers by Social Scientists

In the past thirty years, technological advances have resulted in changes in the way social scientists process and analyze data, and have made
possible types of research which were previously impractical. Before computers, data were hand counted or, as simple machines became available,
transcribed to some form of punched card and processed using mechanical
equipment such as reproducers, collators, and counter sorters. The amount
of data that could be processed and the kinds of analysis that could be
performed were extremely limited.

In its present stage of development, the computer is not only capable of
handling large quantities of data through the use of new storage media,
such as tapes and disks, but is also able to perform extremely complex
analyses in a relatively short time, and relatively cheaply. The computer
is now a tool available to most social scientists. Not only is it available, but its use is no longer limited to the trained computer specialist.
Rather, it is possible for researchers themselves to learn quickly and
easily how to use the computer.

This chapter describes briefly a few important general facts about computers and how data are entered and results extracted. Chapter 2 presents
a general introduction to the research process. Chapters 3 through 6
describe how to use the OSIRIS software package to create, clean, and edit
a data file. Chapter 7 introduces the use of OSIRIS for analysis while
Chapter 8 introduces the notion of OSIRIS structured files and their uses.
No previous knowledge of computers is assumed. The reader need only have
some knowledge of social science data.

1.2   Basic Components of a Computer

Before using the computer, it is necessary to know a few simple, basic
facts about a computer and the way it operates. The orientation in this
monograph is toward large mainframe computers rather than personal computers.

The computer can be divided into four basic components as shown in
Fig. 1.1.

Information, including both data and instructions for performing the
desired operations on the data, is introduced into the memory through input
devices, and stored temporarily in the memory. The central processing unit
(sometimes called the CPU) controls the execution of the instructions upon
the data. Results for the user are output through output devices. These
components are known as the computer hardware, and are described in more
detail below.

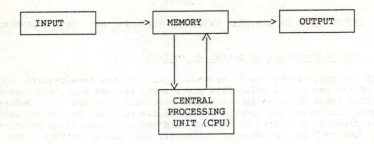

Fig. 1.1   Basic Components of a Computer

1.3   Memory

The memory of a computer is of a certain fixed and limited size, and the
size of the available memory imposes restrictions on the type of data
processing a computer can perform, as well as the amount of information
that can be stored in it at one time. For this reason, the instructions
and data for a particular piece of data processing remain in the memory
only for the duration of that processing; new data and instructions can
then be introduced for the next person's job, overwriting what was there
before.

The size of a computer's memory is usually measured in "K bytes," where
K represents 1024 and a byte is a piece of the memory capable of holding
one character (e.g., a digit or a letter). Thus a 128K computer has 128
bytes x 1024, or 131,072 bytes of memory.

1.4   Input and Output Devices and Media

Information is read into and written out of the memory through input and
output devices: examples of common devices are tape drives, terminals,
floppy disk drives (all of which can be used for either input or output),
card readers (for card input) and card punches (for card output). Information is stored on media: some common media are tape, disk and cards. When
data are in a form that can be read into a computer, they are known as
machine readable data. However, what constitutes "machine readable"
depends upon the capabilities of the input device. For the purposes of
this discussion, only the more common input and output devices and their
associated media will be discussed.

A)   Card Input and Output

The punched card is one medium on which information can be manually
prepared for input to a computer, using a machine called a keypunch.
Each card contains 80 columns. In each column holes can be punched to
represent numbers, letters or other symbols. Each character is
represented by a unique pattern of holes in a single column on a card.
On different keypunches, different conventions determine the
relationship between particular characters and particular configura-

2

tions of holes on the card. The most commonly used convention is called EBCDIC. There are 12 rows on the card. Using only one punch in a column, one can therefore get 12 different characters. In EBCDIC code, these represent the ten digits 0-9 together with the symbols & and -. If there are no holes punched in a column, that column is known as a blank column. A diagram of a card showing the configurations of all the valid EBCDIC characters is given in Fig. 1.2.

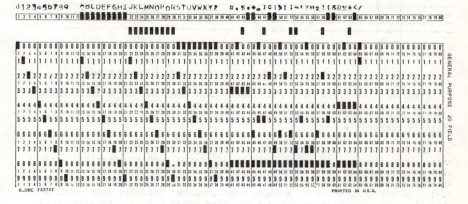

Fig. 1.2 A Punched Card

Information transcribed to punched cards is read into a computer's memory by an input device called the card reader. Information in the memory can be written or punched onto cards by a output device called the card punch to provide card output.

B) Printed Output

Printed output, a medium which can be read directly by the user, is the most necessary form of output from a computer. Printed output is usually written by an output device called the line printer. In recent years devices called page printers, which print on 8 1/2 x 11 paper, have also become available.

C) Magnetic Tape Input and Output

This medium is used for storing large quantities of data compactly. Also, since a computer's memory is of limited capacity, magnetic tape is sometimes used as auxiliary memory for additional work space. Information is magnetically recorded on tracks on the tape (see Fig. 1.3) at densitites ranging from 200 to 6250 characters (or bytes) per inch (bpi). A reel of tape is up to 2400 feet long and if written at a density of 6250 bpi can hold up to 165 million characters of information. Special devices exist for manually recording (punching) data directly to magnetic tape. Normally, however, it is a medium on which the computer itself writes from the memory through a device called the magnetic-tape drive. The same device is also used as an input device for reading the information recorded on a magnetic tape into the computer memory. Fig. 1.3 is a diagrammatic representation of information recorded on a 9-track tape.

3

One Character

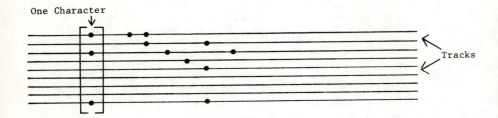

Tracks

Fig. 1.3 Representation of Characters on a 9-track tape.

Different tape drives write different densities and use a different number of tracks. Therefore, once information has been written by a particular type of drive, it must be read by the same kind of drive or one
which is compatible.

Whenever information is written onto a tape, any information previously
existing on the tape is overwritten or destroyed. As a protection against
writing over wanted information, tape drives do not allow anything to be
written unless a special plastic ring is placed in a groove on the tape
reel. In order to write on a tape, most computer installations require
that the user specifically request the ring to be 'in'. Otherwise it is
assumed that information from tapes for a particular task is only to be
read into the memory, leaving the tape untouched. The way this instruction
is given by the user depends upon the installation. Sometimes it might
mean written instructions to the computer operator; sometimes instructions
are punched onto cards in a special format; sometimes instructions are
entered from a computer terminal.

Some of the advantages to tape storage of data over cards are that (i)
information can be read into the memory over 10 times faster (ii) it is a
much more compact form of storage (iii) data on tape is less likely to get
damaged (iv) the order of data cannot get changed.

D) Disk

    Disk is a medium on which information is magnetically recorded on
surfaces in concentric circles or tracks. Disks are written and read by
direct access devices of several kinds. Like tapes, disks are used both
for storing data and as auxiliary memory. The difference between a direct
access device and a tape drive can be compared to the difference between a
record player and tape recorder. In order to read data from the middle of
a disk, one can either scan through the complete disk starting on the outside and working inwards or one can move the read/write head directly to
the desired position. On a tape one has to scan through the complete tape,
starting at the beginning, in order to reach the middle.

E) Terminals

    Terminals are devices used for both input and output; they are
unusual in that they are not associated with a storage medium. There are
many styles of terminals - some are similar to electric typewriters, others
have keyboards and CRT's (cathode ray "television"tubes), and there are

4

other styles as well. Whatever the style, the user "talks" directly to the computer, usually by typing on a keyboard, and the computer "talks" back, usually on a printer or CRT.

1.5   Software

The physical components of a computer described in section 1.2-1.4 above are known as the hardware. A computer cannot function however unless it has instructions in the memory at the time it is called on the perform a task which tell it how to perform that task. The set of instructions to perform a particular task is called a program and the set of programs available for use on a computer is known as the computer's software. Normally programs are stored on a disk and, at the time they are needed, they are introduced into the memory for the duration of the task being performed.

Software can be roughly divided into three classes:

(i)   General purpose programs provided by the installation

(ii) Special purpose programs written for or by a
      particular user for accomplishing some special task

(iii) Software provided by the manufacturer

General purpose programs are programs that have been written to perform a task that many people need to perform; they are written in a general enough way so that undue constraints are not placed on, for example, the format of the user's data or the way the user wants the task performed. Such programs are sometimes called canned programs and are normally stored in program libraries on disk. Each program is assigned a name and when a particular program is required for use, the name is merely specified and the program with that name read from the disk into the computer memory. OSIRIS is a package of about fifty such canned programs designed for processing, manipulating and analyzing social science data. Other such packages used in social science research include SPSS, BMDP, and SAS.

Special purpose programs are often quick and dirty solutions to a particular problem and it is usually the responsibility of the owner to keep a copy on disk, tape or cards.

Software provided by the manufacturer (or sometimes the Computing Center Staff) usually includes a control program. The control program, often called an operating system, controls the execution of user tasks. To do this, it needs information about the task: who is using the computer, which program is being used, which tapes and disk files are required and so on. The user provides the information the control program needs in a special language.

1.6   Operating System Control Language

Different computers use different control programs and different control programs require instructions in different languages. There are three basic types of information that the control program needs from the user: an account number; the name of the required application program; and information about the input and output files required. If an IBM 360/370 computer is being used with the OS or MVS operating system, the control language is known as JCL. Information on JCL commands is given in Appendix H. The control language that will be discussed here is that used for an IBM or Amdahl computer operating under the MTS operating system.

1.7 Michigan Terminal System

Michigan Terminal System commands are prepared by the user and punched onto cards or entered from a terminal. MTS commands to identify the user, to start the OSIRIS package, and to end the job are shown below.

A $SIGNON command signals the start of a job. The user must give his CCID (Computer Center Identification). In addition he may give estimates of computer time required, amount of printed output, etc.

       $SIGNON   1234   T=5

This is a SIGNON command for CCID 1234. (The CCID, 1234 in this example, is assigned by the Computing Center when an account is opened.) The user has supplied a global time limit of 5 seconds: if his job exceeds 5 seconds of Central Processing Unit time the job will be canceled.

Immediately following the $SIGNON command the user must enter his password (a password is assigned by the Computing Center when an account is opened). If the password were LIZARD then

            LIZARD

would be the next card or line from a terminal.

The MTS command to run a program is $RUN, followed by the name of the file where the program is stored. To run OSIRIS at the University of Michigan the command is

       $RUN   ISR:OSIRIS.IV

The MTS command to signal the end of a job is

            $SIGNOFF

MTS commands which are typed on cards must start with a $. The command name should be punched immediately following the $ (no space!). Most commands have one or more required parameters (e.g., a $SIGNON command must include a CCID). Many commands allow optional parameters (e.g., a $SIGNON command may include a time estimate): details of MTS commands can be found in references [8c] and [9a].

At the beginning of this section it was stated that the control program (such as MTS) requires information about input and output data files. In an ultimate sense this is true. However, when using OSIRIS under MTS, the user gives his instructions about files to the OSIRIS monitor which then passes the information to MTS. Discussion of input and output files is therefore postponed to section 1.11, "The OSIRIS Monitor."

6

1.8   Program Control Commands

The Michigan Terminal System commands for the computer's control program are sufficient to schedule a job, name the application program to be used and, if necessary, request the required tapes and disks. If the program being accessed is a general purpose program that can do the task in several ways requiring the user to choose options, then, in addition, the user has to supply control commands for the actual program being used. These can be called program control commands in contrast to job control commands. The complete set of control commands--job control and program conrol--to accomplish a job is known as a setup. The contents of the program control commands is explained in the writeup for the program. Writeups for the programs that are used in the examples in succeeding chapters can be found in the OSIRIS IV Manual [10].

A set of annotated sample setups and computer output can be found in Appendices B and C.

1.9   Batch Processing Versus Time Sharing

Batch processing is the term applied when the user prepares control language, specifying the job to be performed, in some machine readable form (usually lines in a disk file or punched cards), and submits these specifications to the computer. The job is then put in a queue (the position in the queue may depend on certain characteristics of the job through which a priority is assigned). When the job reaches the head of the queue, it is scheduled by the computer's control program and run. The user can then pick up the results. If something was wrong in the original setup, he has to make appropriate corrections, resubmit the job, and then wait for the job to reach the head of the queue and be run again. With larger computers, several jobs can share resources of the computer and be effectively run at the same time. In some systems, the computer's memory is divided up into partitions of fixed sizes. In this case it is usually cheaper and faster to use as small a partition as possible for the particular program that is run. The user must then be aware of the approximate memory requirement of the program being used.

On some computers (time sharing computers), a different mode of operation is also available. With a time sharing computer, one can sit at a terminal (a typewriter like device or a television screen with a keyboard beneath it) which is connected to a computer by telephone line or direct wiring. One types in the job specifications and the job is scheduled and run immediately. The results can be routed to come back to the terminal and if all is not well the user can stop the job, correct the setup and start again immediately. This mode of operation is called interactive because the user can interact with the computer at the time the job is being run.

This text will be geared mainly towards batch processing. However the principles and rationale for doing most tasks is the same whatever the computer system or mode of operation being used. Appendix G describes the interactive use of OSIRIS from a terminal operating under MTS.

1.10 OSIRIS

OSIRIS (the name orginally stood for Organized Set of Integrated Routines for Investigation in Statistics) is the name of an integrated package of computer programs designed for and used at the Institute for Social Research in the processing and analysis of social science data. OSIRIS is particularly useful for datasets resulting from large or complex surveys. OSIRIS requires an IBM 360 or 370 computer, or an IBM-compatible machine such as an Amdahl 470V/7, with at least 150 bytes of available core. The computer must be operated under MTS, the OS, or the MVS operating system. OSIRIS is an integrated package because the control commands required to use each program have a similar structure from one program to another and because there are standard features which are common across most of the programs.

The programs in OSIRIS are roughly divided into two categories: data management and analysis. Data management programs create, correct, copy, and update data files. They usually involve both input and output data: for example, in order to correct an data file, data are read into the memory from an input file, appropriate corrections are made, and corrected data are written onto a new file (the output file) leaving the original input file unchanged. Analysis, on the other hand, usually involves input data files only: data are read into the memory, computations are performed and results are printed.

Often the most time consuming part of computer data processing is the data management. Once data files have been created, checked and corrected, the computer runs required for analyzing the data are relatively easy to set up. Most of the discussion in succeeding chapters therefore concentrates on the data management steps involved in creating data files, and the methods for achieving them making use of OSIRIS data management programs. A brief overview of OSIRIS analysis capabilities is given in Chapter 7 with only two programs (one for descriptive statistics and cross tabulation and one for correlations) described in detail. Complete user documentation for OSIRIS can be found in the OSIRIS IV Manual [10].

1.11 The OSIRIS Monitor

OSIRIS is tied together by the OSIRIS monitor. When the user gives the control program the instruction to run OSIRIS, e.g., in MTS, at The University of Michigan,

$RUN   ISR:OSIRIS.IV

he is invoking the OSIRIS monitor. A particular program in OSIRIS can then be invoked by giving an OSIRIS command to the monitor.[1] The monitor also performs some of the functions normally performed by an operating system, notably the assignment of input and output files. All OSIRIS monitor commands have "&" as a prefix. The OSIRIS program invoked by the & command

---

[1]As noted, an OSIRIS commands starts an OSIRIS program running. The program then does the work; for example, the &ANOVA command starts the ANOVA program, the program which does an analysis of variance. When we imply, as we will, that a command does an analysis or management task, we are ignoring a step (the command calls the program) which is happening inside the computer.

will in turn require program control cards or lines for specifying the type of run.

The example below shows the different types of commands needed for a complete computer job at the University of Michigan. The user's CCID is 5678, his password is SUCCESS. His OSIRIS dataset is stored in disk files named CUDICT4 and CUDATA4; note that he supplies those names on the OSIRIS command card. &ANOVA is a command which does one or more one-way analyses of variance. In this very simple example a single analysis is done, with Variable 22 as the dependent variable and Variable 4 as the control variable.

$SIGNON 5678	*MTS*
SUCCESS	*Command*
$RUN ISR:OSIRIS.IV	*Language*
&ANOVA DICTIN=CUDICT4 DATAIN=CUDATA4	*OSIRIS Command*
ANALYSIS OF VARIANCE-DO MEN AND WOMEN DIFFER -	*Program*
LIVE FOR TODAY	*Control*
*	*Statements*
V=4 DEPV=22	*For &ANOVA*
&END	
$SIGNOFF	*MTS Command*
	Language

1.12 Types of Errors

There are two major types of errors a user can make in preparing a setup--syntax errors and logical errors. Syntax errors are such things as a word being misspelled, a required comma being missing, etc. They can occur in the job control language or in the program control language. Job control language is always checked by the main control program and the error messages the user gets on the printout will be the same whatever application program is being run. Program control language is checked by the program being accessed.

Similarly, logical errors can occur either in the job control or the program control language. Logical errors in job control language are often concerned with a mismatch between information about the data supplied by the user and the actual data. Logical errors in program control cards may mean that the final results are meaningless or may be such that the program being used cannot function with the information it has been given. In the latter case it will terminate with some kind of explanatory error message.

Examples of each type of error are given in Appendix F.

1.13 Summary

To process data by computer, both hardware and software must be available. Hardware consists of input and output devices, memory, and a Central Processing Unit. Software consists of instructions, which, when residing in the memory give the step by step procedures for operating on data. The set of instructions for performing a particular task is known as a program. There are two basic kinds of programs: control programs which control the scheduling and execution of jobs and application programs which are designed to perform a particular task. Application programs may be general

9

purpose--that is they can be used over and over again for different data or special purpose--written for one particular job.

In order to use the hardware and software the user must prepare control statements which give instructions on the job to be performed. Most generally, these instructions are of two basic kinds: instructions to the computer's control program and instructions to the application program itself. In the case of the application program OSIRIS, the later type of instruction can be further broken down: commands to the OSIRIS monitor, which typically invoke a particular OSIRIS program and assign data files, and the program control commands appropriate for that program. The complete set of control statements the user prepares to have the computer perform a particular task is known as a setup.

Chapter 2

INTRODUCTION TO THE RESEARCH PROCESS

2.1 Survey Research

The survey is but one type of research conducted by social scientists. Because it is the major method used by researchers at the Institute for Social Research, the particular examples given will be concerned with data collected from a survey. However, much of the processing that will be discussed is appropriate to data of many kinds and from many sources.

In a survey, a sample of respondents is carefully selected from a larger population of interest; for example, one might select a sample of respondents from the total population of the United States or a sample of potato farmers from the total potato farmer population of Maine. The selection process is usually carefully controlled so that the selection of respondents constitute a representative sample from the larger population. The people in the sample are then administered a questionnaire containing questions of interest to the researcher. Each respondent's answers are then coded and transcribed into machine readable form. Finally, the data are analyzed; the distribution and interrelationships of key variables are examined statistically.

If the sample is drawn in a completely random manner the data collected should reflect the parameters of the total population. Systematic bias, however, can destroy this ability to generalize from the sample to the larger population by misrepresenting each member's chance of being selected into the sample. The classic example of a "biased" sample is one drawn from a city telephone directory and said to represent the population of the entire city. Obviously, many city residents are not listed in the telephone book and therefore never have a chance to enter the sample. The sample is biased because the city residents listed in the phone book have a very different chance of being selected than those not listed. No generalizations to the entire city population can be made. Even random samples from the entire population may be biased if individuals not responding to the survey are systematically different from the respondents. Another sort of complication arises when sampling procedures dictate that a certain type of respondent be overrepresented in the sample compared with the population as whole; in this case the analysis may need to be weighted to adjust for the sample design.

2.2 Questionnaires and Coding

The first step in the survey process is the translation of the researcher's theoretical interests into actual questions and the development of accurate measuring instruments (questionnaires). An example of a questionnaire is given in Appendix A.1. Questionnaire construction and design is an art. Both the respondent and the interviewer must understand the meaning and purpose of the questions asked. In addition the reseacher must be confident that the questionnaire is a valid instrument, that is, the questions are measuring what they are assumed to be measuring. With some of the variables of interest to social scientists--attitudes and behavior patterns--this is a major task.

11

Within the study design some variables are assumed to affect or to predict others. The major relationships between independent variables (predictors) and dependent variables are usually presented in the initial study proposal. These relationships are tested statistically when all the data are in final form.

Most studies conduct pre-tests or pilot studies to test questionnaire design and administration ease. These preliminary tests are usually limited to a small number of respondents and have space allotted to interviewer comments. These comments and the gathered responses are analyzed to see where problems exist. Corrections and improvements are made before sending the final questionnaire into the field situation.

The questionnaire is administered to a sample of respondents of the larger population selected from a listing or other source. The size of the sample is determined by many considerations, for example, the desired precision of the findings, the distribution of subgroups of interest within the general population, and, of course, the available funds to carry out the research. The questionnaire may be administered by an interviewer from a survey agency, either in person or by telephone; it may be mailed to the respondent and self-administered; or, in the case of a secondary data source (e.g., for an analysis of already compiled records), it may be filled in directly by a data analyst or coder. The administration of the questionnaire may be a one time affair or may be repeated at different points in time. (A panel study is one in which the _same_ respondents are reinterviewed.)

Since the late 1970's, telephone interviewing has sometimes been "computer assisted." Computer assisted telephone surveys (also labelled CATI, computer assisted surveys, computer based interviewing) use computer terminals (usually cathode ray terminals) to display questions to an interviewer, who reads them over the telephone to a respondent and then enters the responses obtained to the questions into the terminal. CATI systems route the interviewer automatically to the succeeding questions that are appropriate for the particular respondent. Some CATI systems also schedule the sample cases and assign cases to interviewers, permit the monitoring of interviewers' terminals by supervisors, alter the question wording for particular respondents, randomize the order of questions or of response categories (permitting estimation of order effects on survey statistics), and randomly assign cases to interviewers (permitting estimation of interviewer effects on surveys statistics). The November 1983 issue of Sociological Methods & Research is devoted to articles about CATI.

However the questionnaire is administered, after data are collected they must be coded. Coding is the process of transforming the respondent's verbal answers into numeric values. If a CATI system is used, the coding takes place as the interview progresses. If paper and pencil questionnaires are administered in the field, the questionnaires are usually returned to the survey center for coding. In either case the research staff must have constructed a codebook from the original questionnaire. Each question appears in this codebook followed by a list of possible answers; each possible answer is linked to a particular numeric code value, for example to the question of respondent's sex a male respondent may be coded as '1' and a female as '2'. This codebook is used by the staff of coders to code the questionnaires once they are returned to the survey center. A sample codebook is found in Appendix A.3.

All responses are not as simple as the above male-female dichotomy. The type of responses and the way they are recoded differ from question to question and from study to study.

Four typical types of questions follow:

  (i)   What is your age?_____

        This requires an exact numeric response.

  (ii) How often do you eat meat, never, hardly ever, sometimes, or often?

        This is an example of a question where one of a fixed number of possible answers is allowed. Each possible answer is associated with a numeric code (here 1-4).

  (iii) What is your (main) job? _____

        The response to this question will be the name of the occupation.

  (iv) What do you think is the most pressing problem in our society today? _____

        Here, the respondent is allowed to express feelings in a lengthy verbal response. This type of question is known as "open ended"-- there is no restriction on the type of response that will be elicited.

Numerical responses such as those resulting from question types (i) and (ii) are directly usable for analysis. Non-numeric responses such as received from examples (iii) and (iv) are not amenable to data analysis as they stand. To put them into a form in which analysis can be performed, the data must be translated to numeric values using the codebook constructed for the study. For example, all known occupations have been classified by the bureau of labor and each one is assigned a different numeric code. For an open ended question, the study director can assign numeric codes to types of responses which he thinks will occur. It is the coder's job to fit the actual response to the correct category. If this seem to be impossible for a particular response, the coder may be instructed to make a card. This means that he notes the actual response on a card for later classification. The study director can then look at the cards; if a particular type of response occurs often but was not originally supplied with a unique code, then a new code can be added. If the responses which do not fit into the coding scheme are miscellaneous they would probably be all coded in an "other" category.

Questionnaires can be precoded. This means that numeric codes are assigned to all possible responses on the questionnaire itself and the relevant codes are circled at the time the interview is conducted. In this case the responses need not be translated into code values. The example of such a questionnaire is given in Appendix A.2. Sometimes a few questions on a mainly precoded questionnaire may require coding. In this case the codes can be written directly onto the questionnaire.

After data are in numeric form, they must either be transferred directly from the questionnaire to a computer or converted to some physical form,

13

such as cards, which can be read by a computer. If a CATI system is used,
the data are transferred to the computer essentially simultaneously with
interviewing and coding. Direct data entry (DDE) systems are another
recent development in survey methodology. They are similar to CATI systems
but less elaborate; in DDE systems questionnaires are administered and
coded in a conventional manner and then the coded data are directly entered
into the computer. DDE involves a coder sitting at a terminal and, reading
from the questionnaire, entering the data, by using a typewriter-like
keyboard, directly to the computer. This procedure bypasses code sheets
and punched cards and is being used increasingly. The traditional
procedure for transferring numeric data to a computer is to transcribe the
data to code sheets before entering it into a computer.

Coding sheets are paper with boxes marked off--80 to a line as shown in
Figure 2.1. Each line of the coding form will later be transcribed onto
one punched card or a diskette record.

	1	2	3	4	5	6	7	8		78	79	80
Respondent #1	0	0	0	1	1	0	0	1				
Respondent #2	0	0	0	2	1	0	0	2				
Respondent #3	0	0	0	3	1	0	0	1				
Etc.												

Fig. 2.1 Coding Sheet

The response to each question is transferred to specified boxes or
columns on the coding sheet. Thus the code for state might be recorded in
columns 7 and 8 and the response for sex in column 12. The codes for each
new questionnaire will be transferred to a new line of the coding sheet
with the same columns being used for the same question. Thus, the code for
state would appear in columns 7 and 8 for each questionnaire. Often questionnaires require more than 80 digits of information so that a complete
questionnaire will require several code sheets. The instructions to the
coder, both on the valid codes to be used in coding a particular question
and on the position on the coding sheet or field into which the value is to
be coded, are provided in a codebook, an example of which can be found in
Appendix A.3.

Lines or rows on the code sheet must each be identified in such a way
that it is possible to go back to the code sheet later and know which questionnaire and to which part of the questionnaire that line of figures per-
tains. Thus it is essential that some columns in each line are reserved
for identification purposes. Normally these will include space for the
interview or questionnaire number (sometimes known as case ID) together
with a card identification. Thus if the questionnaire requires four lines
of coding, each row must be identified in specific columns so that one can

refer to the value in these columns and know that a particular row is, say, the third card for that questionnaire. This number, identifying the line of coding, is called the deck number because the information is usually next transferred to a punched card and a collection of punched cards all with the same line number is usually called a deck.

For more information about the coding process, see references [3] and [16].

2.3 Editing

If editing of questionnaires is performed, it usually precedes the coding process. The purpose of editing is to simplify later coding of questionnaires. An editor checks many of the more technical aspects of the questionnaire, for example that instructions were followed and that the interviewer's arithmetic is correct. A major editing task is transforming different units of time, money, etc., into comparable terms. This is a particular problem with many economic variables. A respondent may not be able to answer within the time units given by a question. Consider for example, the question of "How much did you spend on rent during the past year?"--some people may give a flat amount per month to be multiplied by 12 by the interviewer and checked by the editor. Others, however, may report seasonal changes, rate increases and other variations. It is the editor's responsibility to transform all these reports into a single dollar amount per standard unit of time (e.g., a year) for each respondent. Not all studies find editing necessary.

2.4 Machine Readable Data

To transfer data from code sheets to punched cards, diskettes, or magnetic tape a data entry machine is used. A machine called a keypunch, for example, is used to punch cards (see section 1.4 and [8a]). The discussion in the rest of this monograph will use the word card to indicate an 80 character record which may or may not be represented by a physical card.

Since code sheets from the data contain up to 80 columns of information, each line of the code sheet can be transcribed to one punched card. The code identifying the line on the code sheet now identifies the card so that one can pick a card at random from a stack of punched cards and immediately say that this is the nth card for the mth respondent.

The card identification is known as a deck number since usually all cards for the same part of a questionnaire are prepared together. If each questionnaire takes, say, four cards, the one ends up with four decks of cards: one deck of cards representing all the information of the first part of each questionnaire, a second deck of cards representing all information on the second part of the questionnaire and so on. Note that the column location of the case ID and deck number must be the same for all decks.

If the process of transferring codes from questionnaire to code sheet is bypassed and data is keypunched onto cards directly from the questionnaires, then column and deck number for each question should be printed on the questionnaire.

The codebook (or the indications of column numbers on the questionnaire) provide a format for the cards. The card format gives, for a typical card,

15

the positions of the questions. The format of each card with the same deck number is the same.

The questions are known as variables; the value of the response to a particular question varies.

2.5 Missing Data

Data usually contain substantive codes and "missing" data codes. Respondent information is classified as "missing" for various reasons. There are four common reasons for missing data. First, the question asked was "inappropriate" or "inapplicable" for the particular respondent. For example, one does not ask a man what his husband's occupation is. Second, a question may be coded as "not ascertained" because the interviewer forgot to ask the question or the answer was never recorded correctly on the questionnaire. Third, a question may contain a missing data code because the respondent refused to answer a question. And fourth, some studies classify an "I Don't Know" response as a separate missing data category. Normally, when codes are set up for a particular variable, special codes, called missing data codes are assigned to such answers. When the data are analyzed, these responses can be treated differently from other responses or excluded from the analysis. For example, one might want to calculate the mean age for all respondents in the sample; all respondents who refused to answer must be eliminated from such an averaging, even though they may be interesting as a separate category of respondents for other analysis. (See also section 4.4).

2.6 Weighted Data

The respondents that are used for a particular study may be selected in many different ways using sampling techniques. If they are chosen such that there is an equal probability of anyone in the considered population being selected, then each case is treated equally. Sometimes however, one deliberately oversamples certain subsets of population. For example, if one wants enough data to perform separate analysis on people with incomes of $100,000 and above, as well as analyses on the total population, then it might be necessary to deliberately select more rich people. When analyses are performed on the entire population, the responses of these rich people would have to be given less weight in order for the sample to accurately reflect the population. Weights can be assigned to each case in such a way as to reflect the true population when the data are being used for that purpose. Many social science program packages are designed to easily accommodate weighted data in their analysis programs.

2.7 Data Being Used for Examples

The data being used for chapters 1 through 7 of this manual is a modified subset of some data originally generated by Dean Harper and Hanan Selvin for the methodology section meeting of the 1969 American Sociological Association Convention. The purpose of their simulated survey was to determine attitudes towards Campus Unrest. For pedagogical reasons some special variables have been added to the original data in order to give examples of handling certain types of data not in the original file. These new variables, which all appear on the second deck, have no meaning from an

16

analytical standpoint. Also for pedagogical reasons, several errors have been introduced into the data.

The codebook for the data is given in Appendix A.3. Each respondent's data takes two cards or decks. The deck numbers of 10 and 12 respectively are punched in columns 5 and 6 of each card. The respondent is identified by two separate fields (i) a state code punched in columns 7-8 and (ii) a respondent identification number (within state) in columns 10-11. The columns, 7-8, 10-11 and 5-6 taken together uniquely identify a card. The contents of each card are described in the codebook; there, spelled out for each question, is its location on a card, possible codes and their meaning, and an explanation of any special codes. This is an essential document which must be available before processing begins.

For most questions in this dataset, the code 0 means either inapplicable or not ascertained; however the codebook needs to be referred to carefully as this is not so for all questions.

The original data contained twenty-eight questions including the usual demographic variables, four items from the Srole Anomie Scale, eleven attitude items and three items dealing with recent relevant experiences such as whether the respondent has children in college, and political participation. Several attitude items and one relevant experience item have been omitted from the sample data. The contrived questions that have been added give the name of the city of 50,000 or more population nearest to the respondent's home, the number of miles he lives from this city, the length of time it takes to reach the nearest city, and a question about newspaper reading. These special variables provide examples of handling alphabetic variables, decimal points, and multiple responses.

Given that we now have data for a study in punched card form and an associated codebook which formats the cards and gives the possible codes for each variable we are ready to start computer processing.

Four stages of data processing common to the survey research process are: (1) file construction, (2) data cleaning and other manipulation, (3) data reduction and index construction, and (4) analysis or listing of the data. Planning, control, and record keeping are crucial during all stages of data processing. Appendix E contains some suggestions for keeping organized.

2.8 File Construction[2]

After the data are coded and keypunched the file construction process begins. The first step in the file construction process is to check that all our data are present and attached to the correct respondent. This process begins as we sort the data cards. These data cards are read into the computer and a new copy, sorted on the ID number and, within ID, on deck number, is created on tape or disk. Ascending order is usually specified. The resulting data have all cases arranged by ascending order of ID, and within each case all decks in ascending order by deck number.

---

[2] In CATI and DDE systems file construction is part of the system. In some systems these files are constructed so that they are ready for processing by a social science program package.

All the cards or card images for each respondent are now in ascending and contiguous order.

The next step is to examine the structure of our file and document errors such as invalid and duplicate deck numbers, missing decks, etc. After the documented errors have been corrected the user is sure that each respondent has the correct number of data decks and that each card or card image is uniquely identified by a combination of respondent ID's and the correct deck number.

When all data are present and correctly identified, variables must be defined and described. In the early days of computing, most systems required that one specify, within each job, the location of the variables to be used in that run. That is, every time a job was run, the card and column locations of the variables used in the program had to be supplied by the user. For example, one would instruct the computer that there were six decks of information per case and that a certain variable was located on card 5, columns 43-47. This method was time consuming and clumsy, especially since the specification requirements sometimes varied from program to program.

One of the charateristics of OSIRIS (and other modern social science program packages) is that each variable or field is described and defined only once. In OSIRIS this is done when the dictionary is constructed. These definitions are thereafter carried along in a separate file called a dictionary file. Each time an OSIRIS analysis program is executed both the dictionary file and the data file are accessed. Since the same information appears in the same location for each respondent one need only access a variable by number, e.g., Variable 75.

In the file construction process the data is often rearranged to follow the data structure indicated by the dictionary and its variable descriptor statements. If this is done the card image file structure is abandoned for one on which all the data for one respondent appears on one record. Instead of having, for example, three 80 column records per case one respondent will have a record which is perhaps 230 characters long.

Regardless of whether the card image data structure is retained or data for a respondent is rearranged in a single record the combination of the dictionary and associated data file is known as an OSIRIS dataset.

2.9 Data Cleaning[3]

After the dictionary has been constructed, the data are checked. Data cleaning consists of three parts: first, the error is detected; second, the correct value or code is determined by referring to the original questionnaire or codebook; and third, the error is replaced by the correct code on the data file itself.

Errors are introduced from many sources--from coders, keypunchers and data processors themselves. A computer program can be used to read through the data file and detect errors such as wild codes, codes that are not part

---

[3] In some CATI and DDE systems checks on erroneous codes and inconsistencies can be programmed into the computer. If this is done data cleaning takes place as the data are typed into the computer.

of the legitimate coding scheme for a given variable. After all errors are diagnosed and corrections determined by returning to the original interview or coding sheets, these corrections are then incorporated into a new version of the data file.

2.10 Data Reduction and Index Construction

At this point the structure of the data is complete and the substantive values, as far as we can detect, are correct. Technically the data are ready for analysis. However, the researcher may wish to manipulate this "raw" data and create new variables which better measure the dimensions of interest.

These new variables often summarize and restructure the original data. This is done in many ways: by collapsing code categories to reduce the number of subgroups for analysis; by recoding two or more variables together to create a composite index; or by performing arithmetic calculations on certain variables. Examples of the above are: bracketing a two column age variable to create a new variable which codes age as "under 40" or "40 and over"; recoding three attitudinal responses together to create an "efficacy index;" and calculating the average monthly rent from twelve monthly rent rate variables.

It is also possible to create new variables by aggregating across cases as well as variables. For example, one might calculate the average income of a certain county by averaging income across all respondents living in that county.

2.11 Statistical Analysis

Much of the above mentioned variable generation is done with the statistical requirements of certain types of analysis in mind. Certain types of analysis assume certain levels of measurement. These levels refer to the kind of measurement inherent in the numerical codes of a variable.

The most elementary of coding schemes is one in which the code numbers are linked arbitrarily to categories of information. Such a variable is termed nominal or categorical. For example, responses to the question "What kind of car do you own?" are arbitrarily assigned numerical values: Buick might be coded as a 1, Ford as 2, and Oldsmobile as 3. This type of coding scheme limits the type of statistics used to describe a variable. For example, it makes no sense to obtain an average on the above variable. A mean of 2.1 on car types is a meaningless statistic.

Some variables have a meaningful order to their code categories. These are called ordinal variables. For example, responses to a satisfaction question might be assigned numerical codes as follows:

    1. Not at all
    2. A little
    3. Somewhat
    4. Quite a bit
    5. Very much

We know that a code of 4 means more satisfaction than a code of 3. Many attitudinal variables are ordinal variables.

19

A third type is called an interval or continuous variable. In this type of variable the code values follow an incremental scheme. One knows exactly what the gaps between code values mean. That is, an increment in a code has a meaning independent of the value itself. On an income measure we know that $35 is exactly $3 more than $32.

Statistical analysis is concerned with summarizing the properties certain variables exhibit within a sample and establishing the ability to generalize from this sample to the larger population. As we stated above, the statistics chosen for analysis are partially a function of the level of measurement of the variables involved. More will be said about analysis in a later chapter.

Two excellent references for the overall view of processing survey data are [3] and [16].

2.12 Planning and Control of Data Processing

Construction of computer files of survey data in a form suitable for analysis can be a tedious and lengthy process, especially as the first flush of enthusiasm for a survey often fades on completion of the fieldwork. Planning carefully what has to be done, testing out all procedures thoroughly on test data before real processing begins, and existing proper control during all data processing phases extremely important to ensure that the work is streamlined and completed as quickly as possible. Examples of useful kinds of charts and forms for these tasks are shown in Appendix E. Some of the more important points are discussed below.

The first step, while the survey is being planned, is to consider the available hardware and software resources. Generally it is wise to select only a computer which has suitable software available. We will assume here that OSIRIS has been chosen as a package with suitable capabilities and that a computer is available on which OSIRIS is installed. The next step is to design a system making use of the different procedures within OSIRIS to take the data through the various file construction, cleaning and data reduction phases. At the same time it is important to establish naming conventions for the files generated at each stage. A system flowchart is a useful way of representing the procedures to be used and the naming conventions for the files. (See Appendix E for an example.)

Having designed the basic flow of the data, next one must decide whether to process the data in batches as it is coded or whether to wait until all the data are available before starting computer processing. This decision will depend on the quantity of data involved and the speed at which it is being collected. Generally, for surveys of 2000 questionnaires or less, processing in lots is not advisable. For large surveys the work might be completed faster by working with batches of data and by overlapping computer processing with fieldwork/coding. It must be noted however that processing data in lots requires a much higher level of control if utter confusion is not to reign with the multiplicity of files that will be generated.

During the processing phase, good record keeping is essential both to keep track of what has been done (especially important if more than one person is working on the project) and also as a historical record. The latter makes it possible to refer back to results when questions or inconsistencies arise at later stages and is also a useful guideline in making plans and estimates for future surveys. The following types of records are recommended and relatively easy to keep.

1. Computer runs

   Here one records a run identification of some kind along with the name of the program and the input and output files used, the cost or CPU to time consumed, the date, the outcome and possibly a brief verbal description of the purpose of the run. For completeness, records may be kept for all runs including those which fail.

2. Tape/data set records

   For each data set created, the dataset name should be recorded along with the record length, number of records, date and a reference back to the run that created it. A short verbal description of the contents is also useful. If datasets are being stored on tape, this record should be kept on a tape by tape basis with the file numbers of each dataset also noted.

3. Computer printout

   Computer printout from all processing steps must be kept for easy reference as queries arise. It should be filed according to run identification and clearly labelled. However, it can get fairly bulky and difficult to manage and it may not be possible to store all in a convenient place. An alternative might be to file only listings of the control commands near at hand which are often sufficient to resolve problems and the more bulky output (clearly labelled with the run identification) in a different location.

   The discipline of keeping good records which are vital for successful data processing is hard to maintain. Some of the work can however be automated. The Science and Technology Policy Division of UNESCO for example made a modification to OSIRIS so that a unique identification is automatically assigned to each run, two copies of the control commands are always listed (one for local filing and the other for filing with the results) and in addition a record of the run is stored on disk. This system serves the dual purpose of automatically kept run records and the means to store control card listings for easy retrieval separately from main printout.[4] See also the OSIRIS &DOC command.

The last point to mention in this section is the question of backups. Many files are generated during the processing and cleaning of survey data most of which are transitory in nature. For example, a checking run is made on a file which is then updated with corrections and a new file generated. The checking run is repeated and another new file generated incorporating additional corrections. It is neither necessary nor desirable to keep all intermediate files – it leads to confusion and

---

[4]UNESCO/STP OSIRIS Run Documentation System, March 1975

to wasteful use of tapes or disk space. However, for safety,
the file generated by one step should always be retained until
the next but one step has successfully run. This gives
'grandfather, father, son' versions of the data. At the subsequent step (the creation of the grandson), the grandfather
can be purged or overwritten. In addition to this system,
certain files should be kept permanently. These will serve
as an emergency resource in case major data processing errors
are detected or final files inadvertently destroyed. Such
files are normally those resulting from the completion of
a particular phase. For example, one might keep the original
raw data as it was entered into the computer, the data after
all cleaning steps have been completed and the final file of
variables generated for analysis purposes. After the processing is complete, only these key files need to be kept but
a copy of each should be made for security.

2.13 Archiving data

When all preliminary results from a survey have been obtained and
a report written there may still be interesting material in the
data that has not been fully exploited. In addition, the data
might form a useful comparison or supplement to other surveys.
Normally therefore it is desirable to keep data for a length
of time in a suitable form for further analysis.

The important points to note here is that machine readable data
without associated documentation describing it is almost unusable.
The documentation advisable to keep is at minimum the following:

- the questionnaire
- instructions to interviewers if any
- details of how the sample was selected
- the editing instructions
- the coding manual
- the system used for cleaning the data and any decisions
  made that affected the contents
- rules for constructing variables or indexes from the
  original variables
- simple frequency distributions of all original variables

If the main analysis file contains variables constructed from the
original questions, then at minimum two computer files should be
retained - the cleaned raw data file and the file containing the
constructed variables.

Chapter 3

INITIAL DATA FILE PREPARATION

3.1 Introduction

Most of the data processing principles discussed in this text apply
equally well to disks or tapes - or, for that matter, to drums or film.   In
general, the focus in this text will be on data stored on disk.   In this
chapter, however, procedures for disk and tape will be described separately, partly because it provides an opportunity for a few more general
remarks on these two most common mediums.   If the data file consists of one
logical record per case on disk or tape, much of the material in this chapter may be skipped.

If the data have been punched on cards, the first step in computer data
processing is to make a copy of these cards on to some other, more convenient, medium such as disk or magnetic tape.   There are several reasons
for not using cards, e.g.,

   a) Cards are bulky and hard to handle.
   b) Reading data from cards is much slower than reading data
       from tape or disk.
   c) Cards can be easily dropped, lost, shuffled, or damaged in
       handling.

After cards have been copied to tape or disk, the next process is to
check that all the cards in the tape or disk file belong to the correct
study and that there are no duplicate or missing cards.   For this check to
be performed, the data must first be ordered so that if one respondent's information is contained on more than one card, all the records for that
respondent are physically next to each other.

There are therefore three processes in preliminary data file preparation: (i) copying cards to disk or tape (ii) sorting data (iii) checking
for missing duplicate and bad cards.   The way these three steps are accomplished using the OSIRIS package of general purpose programs on an IBM
360/370 or an Amdahl computer operated under the MTS system is shown below.

3.2 Copying Cards to Disk

When the data for a study are transcribed to disk they are placed in
what is known as a file.   At most computer installations each user may have
private files on disk which belong to him and which may be used only by
him, unless he gives others permission to access them.   There are two types
of private files, permanent and temporary.   At the University of Michigan
permanent files are created by the user by giving an MTS command, $CREATE;
they exist until they are explicitly destroyed - often for weeks or months.
The user makes up a name for the file when he creates it: the name for a
permanent private file should start with a letter or a number and not ex-
ceed twelve characters.   Temporary files can be either created explicity
(e.g., using $CREATE as above) or implicitly on first mention; they exist
only until the user signs off.   The user makes up names for temporary files
too: at The University of Michigan temporary files must have a "-" (i.e.,
minus) as their first character.

A possible first MTS command for the copy cards to disk job is:

$CREATE   CUDATA

this command would set aside one page of disk, naming it CUDATA. A page of
disk holds about 50 cards or 4000 characters. There is also some overhead
for each file. (Formulas for calculating file size are given in [9a].) If
a page proves not to be enough when the cards are actually read in, the MTS
control program will automatically expand the file (within limits). It is
neater (and slightly cheaper) to estimate in advance the number of disk
pages needed and to create the file correctly in the first place ("up" your
estimate slightly if in doubt). Although 3P would be good guess, for the
data in Appendix A.3 the ideal command is:

$CREATE   CUDATA   SIZE=4P

There are different ways to copy cards to disk. With MTS, the simplest
way is to use the MTS command $COPY as follows:

$COPY   *SOURCE*   filename

"*SOURCE*" is the name set by MTS for the card reader; filename is the name
of the disk file where you want the data to end up.

A complete cards-to-disk copy job might look as follows:

```
$SIGNON     SDM3
LIZARD
$CREATE     CUDATA     SIZE=4P
$COPY     *SOURCE*     CUDATA
    .
    .          data cards
    .
$ENDFILE
$SIGNOFF
```

The cards to be copied should be placed directly after the $COPY command.
The $ENDFILE signals the last of the cards. If your card to disk job
works, and it probably will, you will never have to use the cards again.
Although the commands above are, in their details, peculiar to the MTS control program, they are representative of the sort of facility offered by
any operating system.[5]

3.3 Copying Cards to Tape

When the data for a study are transcribed onto tape they form what is
known as a file or datafile (just as when they are transcribed to disk).
There may be more than one file of data on a tape. One file on a tape can
be distinguished from another by a dataset header label which contains the
name and some other descriptive information about the data and which appears in front of the appropriate dataset. One tape is distinguished from

---

[5]The result of this cards-to-disk copy job is stored in a permanent file
named CUDATA on University of Michigan account (CCID) SDM3. The data may
be read or copied from that file.

24

another by a volume label which is written at the beginning of the tape and contains the tape's number (volume serial number).

Tapes do not have to be labelled. However, if they are not there are no machine checks that the correct tape is being used or that the correct dataset on that tape is being accessed. One string of numbers on a tape looks like any other string of numbers and there is no way for the computer to check that it is using the correct data when the user requests a particular tape and file. It is recommended therefore that labelled tapes always be used. They will be assumed in this text.

New tapes are completely blank and a volume label must be written to them using a program designed for that purpose. This is called tape initialization; the volume label (volume name, volume serial number, are equivalent terms) inscribed magnetically at the beginning of the tape is henceforth the signal to the computer that it is a labelled tape. If a tape has existing data it will already have been intialized; if all the existing data is to be discarded it may be reinitialized. Intialization effectively empties a tape of any existing data - so, except for brand new tapes, it should be used with caution.

At the University of Michigan, computing Center staff always performs the intialization of brand new tapes; however users can reinitialize tapes themselves, by using the MTS $CONTROL command. At some installations users run a tape intialization program themselves - typically it takes just a card or two. Once a tape contains a magnetically inscribed volume label, a request to have that tape mounted will cause the computer system to check that the label on the tape the operator mounts matches the label the user specified in his mount request. If the two do not agree, the job will not run.

A tape must be mounted on a tape drive in order to be used. An example of the MTS command to mount the tape with volume serial number 9129 which is physically stored in the Computing Center rack number C1569A might be:

        $MOUNT   C1569A   9TP   *T*   VOL=9129

Here 9129 is a 9-track tape (see section 1.4.c). "*T*" is a name (what appears between the asterisks is choosen by the user) which will be used by the user to refer to the tape once it has been mounted. The rack number, device type (9TP), and name must be given in that order.

Before a tape can be written on, the operator must physically insert a plastic ring (rather like a mason jar ring) into the hub of the tape reel. To request "ring in" for tapes so that they can be written on the user puts RING=IN or WRITE=YES on the $MOUNT command. Another possible parameter for the $MOUNT command has to do with the number or name written manually on the outside of the tape reel: if that number is different from the internal number or name (inscribed magnetically), then the external number must appear at the end of the $MOUNT command enclosed in primes. Another possible $MOUNT command for tape 9129 is shown in Fig. 3.1.

$MOUNT	C1569A	9TP	*OUT*	VOL=9129	RING=IN	'CU1'
	storage rack (computer operator goes here to find tape)	it is a nine track tape	name user will use to refer to tape in later steps of this job	volume number writ- ten in magnet- ism (comp- ter checks this)	allows tape to be writ- ten on dur- ing this job	identi- fication on out- side of reel

Fig. 3.1. Sample MTS $MOUNT Command

We turn now to the actual copying. To create a copy of cards on tape, the cards are read through the card reader into the memory and a copy writ- ten out onto tape, to form what is known as a card image file on tape. For this process decisions must be made concerning how the card images are to be written to tape. As explained above, a tape that has had a volume label written to it is known as a labelled tape. A file or dataset on a labelled tape is structured as shown in Fig. 3.2. At the beginning there is a header label containing the name of the file and other descriptive information. This is followed by a special character called a tape mark which is an end signal to the tape drive. The data then follows in blocks. Between each block there is an inter-block gap. At the end of the data there is another tape mark followed by a trailer label which contains all the same informa- tion as the header label and, in addition, a count of the number of blocks in the file. Within each block of information there may be several records. While dealing with card image data, each card image constitutes one record. The more records that are packed into one block, the less physical tape and the less computer time in processing the data is used (because of fewer interblock gaps).

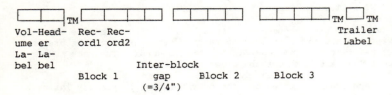

Vol-Head-   Rec- Rec-   Trailer
ume er   ord1 ord2   Label
La- La-
bel bel   Inter-block
          Block 1   gap   Block 2   Block 3
                         (=3/4")

Fig. 3.2. Structure of the First Data File on a Labelled Tape

When the dataset is first written, the size of the record and the block must be specified, either through use of a format keyword on the $MOUNT or $CONTROL commands (see section 1.6, [8b], and [9c]), or if the program being used allows it, through use of parameters in the program control cards. At the University of Michigan, blocksizes from 8,000 to 16,000 characters are good choices for efficiency. This is a trade off between efficient tape, disk, and computer time usage and the amount of computer memory needed for processing the data (enough memory to accomodate a com- plete block of data is required by the system).

There are many different programs that can be used for copying cards to tape. The example given below uses the MTS $COPY command.[6]

```
$MOUNT C1659 9TP *TAPE* VOL=9129
RING=IN DSN=CUDATAl FORMAT=FB(8000,80) FILE=*1*
$COPY *SOURCE* *TAPE*
        .
        .    data cards
        .
$ENDFILE
```

The control cards given above will copy the card data to tape, creating what is known as a card image file. The $MOUNT card describes the file that is to be written. In this case a file with name CUDATAl is being written to tape number 9129; the record characteristics are specified with the FORMAT keyword which says here that the records will be of fixed length and blocked (FB), 100 cards will be written in each block (8000) and each record has a length of 80 (80). The cards are to be written in the first file of the tape (FILE=*1*). (This assumes there is nothing of value anywhere on the tape; writing on a tape destroys everything further out on the tape.) The minus at the end of the first line of the $MOUNT command is a continuation signal. (On an MTS command, when the input is from   cards, the continuation signal, if required, must be in column 80 of the card; in all other cases a continuation signal may just be the last character of the card or line.) The $COPY command copies from *SOURCE*, the name set by MTS for the card reader, to *TAPE*, the name set by the user for referring to his tape. The $ENDFILE simply signifies the last of the cards.

When data are written to a labelled tape, a dataset header label is automatically written in front of the data. This header label will contain the dataset or file name, as specified on the $MOUNT command which described the file when it was written, along with characteristics of the records in the file--whether they are fixed or variable length, whether they are blocked, and the record length and block length. When the data are accessed later for reading, the user has to specify (among other things) the tape number (on the $MOUNT) and the dataset name or file number or both (as part of the OSIRIS command --CUDATAl or FILE=1 for this example). If both the dataset name and file number are given the computer system will check that the dataset name given by the user is the same as that in the dataset header label for the specified file. If the two do not agree, the job will terminate. The data can therefore only be accessed if the dataset name is accurately known by the user. If the name is mislaid, a special program must be used which will print the contents of the labels on the tape.[7]

If the dataset name specified by the user does agree with that written on the tape, then the data can be accessed using the record characteristics with which they were written and which are now part of the dataset header label. In some special circumstances, these record characteristics can be overridden by respecifying them on the $MOUNT command. For example, when cards are copied to tape, the resulting card images on the tape always have

---

[6] In this and future examples, the initial $SIGNON and password and final $SIGNOFF will be omitted.

[7] The procedure used at the University of Michigan for doing this is to $RUN *LABELSNIFF (see Volume 2 of the MTS Manual [9b]).

a fixed record length of 80 characters. In order to treat two cards as one
record, one can specify a record length of 160 on the $MOUNT command when
reading the file. This specification will override what is in the label
and the data will be accessed by the program that is being used in units of
160 characters instead of 80 characters at a time. This can only be done
if the actual blocksize of the data is an exact multiple of the new record
length.

3.4 Sorting Data

In order to check that the correct number of cards exist for each
respondent the data must first be sorted so that all cards for one respondent are contiguous. Sorting is usually performed by a computer; a sort
program is used which reads a dataset into the computer's memory, rearran-
ges the records and creates a new file sorted according to the user's
specifications.

Even if there is only one deck per case sorting is recommended. Later
in processing we will come across programs that operate correctly only when
the data are sorted. For example, many programs that involve matching data
from more than one source require that all files be sorted the same way on
match variables.

Sorting is performed by arranging records in order according to the
values in certain parts of the record, known as the sort fields or ID
fields. Our Campus Unrest data have two ID fields and a deck number that
uniquely identify each card. The first ID is state (the major sort field);
within each of the five states in our sample each respondent has a two
digit respondent ID (the minor sort field). To sort all data for each case
into numerical order one must sort on three fields: state (columns 7-8);
within state on respondent ID (columns 10-11); and within ID on deck number
(columns 5-6). Note that each ID and the deck number are located in the
same columns across all data cards. This is an extremely important requirement of most data processing systems. There is no way of sorting unless identification fields are located in the same columns across data
cards.

Sorting our records on ID's and deck number produces a file with all
case cards grouped in order and all cases ordered numerically. Records can
be sorted in ascending or descending order. All of the following examples
assume ascending sequence.

If data contain non-numeric characters, for example, dashes, blanks or
alphabetics, it is important to know the IBM character sequence. This sequence is used in virtually all sorting programs. From lowest to highest,
the order is: blanks, special characters (&, -), alphabetics and numerics.
Note that a blank is not equal to a zero; they are very different characters. If you are sorting a two digit field,'b̸4' is lower than '01'.
Figure 3.3a shows a list of characters before and after being sorted in ascending order.

Figure 3.3b presents a few Campus Unrest data records before and after
sorting.

Unsorted	Sorted	
0	ƀ	low
+	+	
7	A	
A	0	
ƀ	7	high

Fig. 3.3a. Sort Order of Miscellaneous Characters

Before Sorting			After Sorting		
Card	State	ID	Card	State	ID
5-6	7-8	10-11	5-6	7-8	10-11

Card	State	ID		Card	State	ID
10	1	01		10	2	03
10	2	01		12	2	01
10	1	02		10	2	01
12	1	01		12	1	02
10	2	03		10	1	02
12	1	02		12	1	01
12	2	01		10	1	01
(Top of Deck)				(Top of Deck)		

Fig. 3.3b. Card Image Data: Before and After Sorting

The OSIRIS command used for sorting is &COPYSORT. The details of this
command and several examples of its use can be found in the OSIRIS IV
Manual [10]. In the first of the following sample setups the input data
file is on disk, in a file named CUDATA. The sorted output file is written
to a new disk file, named CUSORTED. (It is a general OSIRIS rule, disk or
tape, any command, that input and output files must be distinct.)

```
$CREATE  CUSORTED SIZE=4P
$RUN ISR:OSIRIS.IV
&COPYSORT SORTIN=CUDATA SORTOUT=CUSORTED -
  S=CH,A,7,2,CH,A,10,2,CH,A,5,2 REC=200
&END
```

The input and output files are specified on the &COPYSORT command; the
specific files for this job, CUDATA and CUSORTED, are assigned to SORTIN
and SORTOUT, input and output names set by OSIRIS for &COPYSORT. The sort
fields definition must follow the input and output assignments and begins

29

with "S=." (The sort fields definition appears on the same card as the
&COPYSORT command itself; note the minus indicating card continuation in
the example above.) Following S=, the user provides a list of the fields
he wants to sort on. Each field specification is composed of four elements: the storage mode of the sort field (ours is character, CH, which is
usual), the desired output sort order (A, for ascending), the first column
of the sort field, and the field width. In the above example we specified
the three fields necessary to put our data file in order: state, respondent
ID, and card number. Thus we have twelve elements following the S=
(3x4=12). Following the sort fields definition is the REC= parameter; this
parameter is an estimate of the number of records to be sorted (if in
doubt, err upwards); if this parameter is omitted it defaults, i.e., is set
by the program, to 5000.

CUSORTED is a disk file written by OSIRIS. OSIRIS always writes
"blocked," "labelled" disk files. These terms have the same general meaning as they do for tapes (see section 3.3); usually it is not necessary for
the user to worry about the format of OSIRIS disk files.

An example setup for the same job, but tape to tape, would be as follows:

```
$MOUNT C6656C 9TP *IN* VOL=CU1; -
C6657C 9TP *OUT* VOL=CU2 RING=IN
$RUN ISR:OSIRIS.IV
&COPYSORT SORTIN=*IN*(DSN=CUDATA) -
SORTOUT=*OUT*(DSN=CUSORTED,FILE=1) -
S=CH,A,7,2,CH,A,10,2,CH,A,5,2 REC=200
&END
```

In section 3.3, copying cards to tape, DSN, FORMAT, and FILE information
was given on the $MOUNT command. When using OSIRIS, these characteristics
of a file are given in parentheses following (no space!) the particular input or output assignments. In the above example an output format is not
specified - this because OSIRIS takes care of specifying formats. In
&COPYSORT and some other commands, the user may optionally specify a blocksize, in effect overriding OSIRIS's choice.

Copying data to disk or tape (described in the previous section) and
sorting (described in this section) can be accomplished in a single step.
The way to do this is described in the data management section of the
OSIRIS manual. Combining the steps is sensible if the dataset is small (so
that rereading the cards, because, say, an error in the sort fields
definition, would not be daunting) or if the user is experienced (an error
in the sort step is unlikely).

3.5 Checking for Completeness of Data - The OSIRIS &MERCHECK Command

Having sorted our card image data the next step is to check the completeness of our data. We know that we should have two decks of data for
each Campus Unrest respondent, the first numbered 10 and the second 12.
This assumption is checked by the OSIRIS &MERCHECK command. In the OSIRIS
system each case is required to have the same number of decks. Even if
some decks are deliberately missing for certain cases, dummy decks must be
added to the file. &MERCHECK performs this function also.

30

This program is only necessary when one has multiple cards per case. If the user has only one deck per case, merge checking is unnecessary, although it can be used to check for incorrect sort order and duplicates.

&MERCHECK checks that each case has the correct number of decks and that these decks are numbered correctly. Note that this program checks the structure of each case; it does not examine substantive codes other than ID's, deck numbers, and a constant, if there is one.

&MERCHECK examines the cards comprising each case and documents errors in sort order, missing or duplicate cards, and extraneous cards. If our respondent number 02 from New York has two cards, one numbered 10 and a second numbered 13, this is an error we want to know about and correct. Chances are good that the card 13 is a keypunch error and should be 12. There are many sources of error in processing a data file; some errors are more complex than others. &MERCHECK is the first step of the error detection process. It checks that all data cards are present and in correct order for each respondent.

&MERCHECK produces a listing of cases with errors and the appropriate diagnostic messages. It also creates an output file containing complete cases--complete in the sense of having the correct number of cards per case. It is possible to instruct &MERCHECK to insert a card if one is missing. Unless otherwise specified, i.e.,the PAD= option is supplied, this card will be filled with nines except for case and deck ID numbers. Within the program it is possible to specify which cards to keep if duplicate cards are encountered, and how the error cases are to be output and documented. It is then up to the user to correct these structural errors.

Two different procedures for handling error cases follow. These are shown schematically in Figure 3.4. In our sample &MERCHECK setup we will use method A. The output file will contain two cards for every input case with a valid ID. Error cases are kept within the data, to be corrected at some later date. For example, if a Campus Unrest case is missing deck 10, &MERCHECK will output two cards; one which is all pad characters except for the valid ID and card number '10' and the second containing card '12' data as it was input. The assumption is that the pad characters on card '10' will be replaced later by appropriate data. This method is frequently used with small datasets such as ours.

The second method involves writing to the output file only "good" cases, those diagnosed as being totally free from format errors. Bad cases are directed to a different file (or to the card punch). If the error cases are written or punched out the errors are corrected by hand, and &MERCHECK is run again on the error cases. This method is advisable for large datasets; the corrected data are reinserted using a &COPYSORT procedure and further data cleaning is done on the entire file.

The &MERCHECK example below follows the general OSIRIS job setup outlined in section 1.11. The OSIRIS IV Manual [10] program writeup for &MERCHECK explains the particular program control cards for &MERCHECK. The file containing the input data is assigned to DATAIN; the file for the output data is assigned to DATAOUT. The program control cards consist of: a label statement, up to 100 characters in length, which is used to title the run; a parameter statement which specifies the options selected for this run; and a special set of statements, deck descriptions, which are specific to &MERCHECK.

31

```
$CREATE CUMERGED SIZE=4P
$RUN ISR:OSIRIS.IV
&MERCHECK DATAIN=CUSORTED DATAOUT=CUMERGED
CHECKING MERGE OF CAMPUS UNREST DATA
PRINT=ALL MAXP=2 IDCOL=(7-8,10-11) MAXE=20 DUPK=1 CONS='400' CLOC=78
DECK=10 IDLOC=5 PAD='-
   10II0II 0099000000000000000000                              40-
0'
DECK=12 IDLOC=5 PAD='-
   12II II                       999999  9999999              40-
0'
&END
```

Options that control the processing and documentation of cases with errors, duplicate decks, etc., are specified on the parameter statement. It
is not always necessary to specify the options one wants because of program
defaults (a default is a value assigned by the program if the user does not
specify an option choice). For example we need not have specified the
DUPK=1 option, the sequential number of the duplicate to keep when duplicate deck records occur. The DUPK default, 1, suits our choice. Sometimes
a default is selected by omission: by not specifying write we have accepted
the default of not writing out error cases in a separate file. By specifying MAXP=2, that up to two decks may be padded and still retain the case,
we have insured that two cards will be output to the "good" file for every
unique ID.

If duplicate records are encountered, the first one will be kept. Any
choice of which duplicate to keep is a gamble. One must check duplicates
at a later point. A duplicate record with &MERCHECK refers only to the
repetition of ID and deck numbers; no reference is made to any other data
appearing on the record. Duplicates refer only to duplicate ID's, not
necessarily duplicate data. Padded decks must also be checked at a later
point.

In our setup a limit of twenty cases with errors is set (MAXE=20); as
soon as this number is exceeded the job will stop. This limit is usually
set after considering both the number of errors one expects and the reason
for running &MERCHECK. For example, if one deck is known to be missing
from a large number of cases and the &MERCHECK command is being used to pad
in these missing decks, the maximum number of cases with errors may need to
be equal to the total number of cases. On the other hand, if there is no
padding involved and the data should be fairly clean, many users set the
maximum to somewhere between a quarter and a half of the total number of
cases. With such a limit, error messages generated because of program control card misspecifications will be diagnosed without running through the
entire dataset. On the other hand, if the errors are frequent and
legitimate (for example a complete deck is missing from the data file) the
output will supply enough information to make the necessary adjustments.

Two of the parameters deal with the presence of a constant on each of
our data cards. This unchanging number is often the study number or some
other identifying digits. The Campus Unrest data has a constant, the study
number, 400, beginning in column 78.

Following the parameter card there must be one deck specification statement for each deck. A deck ID and its beginning column must appear on the
specification card (e.g., DECK=10 IDLOC=5). In addition, values to be used
for padding may be specified using the PAD= keyword. If one expects miss-

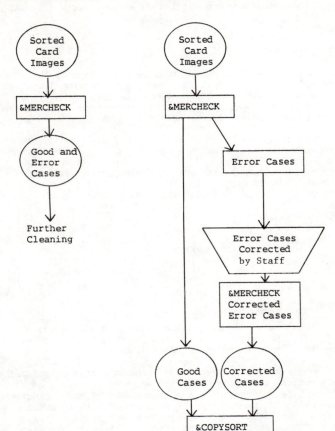

Method A

Small data files

Method B

Large data files

Fig. 3.4 &MERCHECK Methods

ing data on certain cases, specifications of say, 0's or 8's (whatever the missing data code is for each variable) might be more appropriate than 9's, which are the default for everything except deck number and case ID. In the example above actual missing data codes--see the codebook in Appendix A.3--are used for padding. The PAD keyword is spread over three cards in the example. This is not necessary and admittedly awkward; it does however allow for easy checking that missing data codes are assigned to the correct columns.

The output file written by &MERCHECK always follows the structure outlined by the deck specification statements. In our Campus Unrest example
any case missing a deck will have a record inserted that has the proper
deck number, a case identification, and missing data codes for the variable
values.

3.6 &MERCHECK -Tape Example

The same job for data stored on tape is shown below. The only thing new
in the following setup is that the tapes for the sort in section 3.4 have
been ping-ponged, the sort input tape (CU1) is now the output tape, the
sort output tape (CU2) is the input tape. On the output tape (CU1) we
write in file two so as not to destroy the original raw data.

```
$MOUNT C6657C 9TP *IN* VOL=CU2; -
C6656C 9TP *OUT* VOL=CU1 RING=IN
$RUN ISR:OSIRIS.IV
&MERCHECK DATAIN=*IN*(DSN=CUSORTED) DATAOUT=*OUT*(DSN=CUMERGED,FILE=2)
CHECKING MERGE OF CAMPUS UNREST DATA
PRINT=ALL MAXP=2 IDCOL=(7-8,10-11) MAXE=20 DUPK=1 CONS='400' CLOC=78
DECK=10 IDLOC=5 PAD='-
      10II0II 0099000000000000000000000                               40-
0'
DECK=12 IDLOC=5 PAD='-
      12II II                    999999  9999999                      40-
0'
&END
```


3.7 Merging New Cases into the File

Since the Campus Unrest data file is small we have kept all cases, good
and bad, with a valid ID. Our assumption is that the data for the error
cards will be corrected at a later point in processing.

If, on the other hand, the error cases are written to a file or punched
out by the &MERCHECK program they must be corrected before they can be
added to the good case file produced by the original &MERCHECK. Correction
cards for error case cards are produced by first checking with relevant
interview or code sheets and then keypunching replacement cards. It is
then wise to rerun &MERCHECK on these cases. That way the data processor
can be sure that the corrected cases are, in fact, complete cases.

The next step would be to combine our original good case file with our
now correct, smaller file of corrected error cases. This process is shown
diagramatically under method B in Figure 3.4. Note that two files are
being combined; if the first file has 96 cases and the second file has 4,
our new file will have 100 cases. The &COPYSORT command can be used to
combine the files by concatenating (chaining together) the SORTIN files.[8]

---

[8]Under MTS concatenation can be accomplished by giving the names of the
files connected by plus signs (e.g., SORTIN=CUMERGED+FIXED).

34

3.8 Summary

In this chapter we have described the preliminary steps in preparing our data file. Our data cards have been sorted into a meaningful order and checked for completeness. At the end of this process we can be confident that the structure of our dataset is correct: each case contains the correct number of cards and the card numbers are accurate. At the same time it is likely that we have uncovered some problems with the data. The output from a &MERCHECK must be examined very carefully --see, for example, the &MERCHECK printout in Appendix C. For our small dataset we elected to keep the error cases in the same file with the good cases. The error cases will in due course be corrected. However the correction procedure will be simpler if we first create an OSIRIS dataset. That will be the next step.

Chapter 4

CREATING AN OSIRIS DATASET AND STANDARD OSIRIS CONTROL CARDS

4.1 Describing Data

In previous processing described in this manual, the location of data fields or variables was indicated in different ways. In the &COPYSORT command, fields are indicated by their starting location and field width; in &MERCHECK the IDCOL keyword and the IDLOC keyword use special conventions to identify ID and deck positions. Ten or fifteen years ago, systems often used card and column numbers to designate relevant variables. A much better system is one where all variables are defined initially and these definitions are carried along for use in future computer runs. With the OSIRIS 'dictionary' this is in fact what occurs. After creating a dictionary for one's data, each variable's name, number, disk or tape location(s), and missing data codes, as well as some other information about it, are carried along in a separate machine readable file, called a dictionary file.

The dictionary file is an identifying feature of the OSIRIS system. It accompanies a data file and is a repository of information about the variables in the data base. This dictionary is itself a file of records, one 80 character record per variable, containing descriptive information. When one accesses Variable 57, for example, in an OSIRIS program the dictionary is searched to determine the position of the variable within the data record. Other information, such as the name of the variable, is also retrieved from the dictionary and is printed out to make computer printout easier to read.

Dictionaries are initially created by the OSIRIS &DICT command (see sections 4.2-4.6). Once data are described by an OSIRIS dictionary certain standard OSIRIS features become available. These are discussed in sections 4.9-4.13.

Other information from the codebook may also be included in an OSIRIS dictionary such as the actual wording of questions asked, the code categories allowed and so on. In this case we get what is known as a 'machine readable code book'.

4.2 OSIRIS Dictionaries

A dictionary file describes a particular file of data. Together the two files are often referred to as a "standard" OSIRIS dataset. This term is somewhat misleading in that there is nothing special about the data involved; the term merely signifies that these two files, the dictionary and the data file, are used together by most OSIRIS programs.

The &DICT command is used to create dictionaries from scratch. Along with the command, and a couple of standard control cards, the user supplies special statements, variable descriptor statements, which instruct the computer how to interpret the data file. Each variable descriptor record supplies information about one variable and specifies its location on the data file. Usually, the data file is, as it is in our Campus Unrest example, a sorted, merchecked, card image file; although we shall assume in the following discussion that the data are in card image form that last requirement is not strictly necessary (if, for example, raw data had been typed

37

into the computer from a terminal rather than entered on cards the record lengths might all be 60 columns rather than 80 columns). On the other hand, as will become evident as we discuss building a dictionary, it is foolhardy to use a dictionary with data which is not sorted and merchecked.

Consider again our Campus Unrest data. Each case consists of two records, each record being 80 characters long.

```
             0000000001111111111222222222233333        778
Column       12345678901234567890123456789012341   etc.        890
```

First Case

```
            110 11 121239&13294 73022212111            400
             12 1  1DETROIT              55 15 1212213    400
```

Second Case

```
            210 12 211282711265 01111211121            400
             12 1  2KALAMAZOO             32 10 1321133    400
```

Fig. 4.1 Card Image Data With Two Decks per Case

The identification variables, columns 7-8 (state) and 10-11 (respondent ID), appear on both cards; we will need to describe them only once each in the dictionary. Likewise the constant (400) will need to be described only once (or not at all) in the dictionary. The deck number, which has served its purpose, will not need a variable description statement at all. Also note that deck 10 is blank from columns 35 through 77 on all cases and deck 12 contains blanks for columns 45 through 77. This blank space need not be described in our dictionary. For convenience, we may wish to group certain variables together; for example, we might group the city and community variables together. In short, what &DICT will do for the Campus Unrest Data is make a dictionary for it, which describes the variables for one case; since all cases have the same variables, in the same locations, describing one case describes them all.

The output dictionary will contain the following information for each variable (see Fig. 4. 2): variable number, type of variable (numeric or alphabetic), name, group (always 0 unless it is a structured file), starting position in data record and field width, number of implied decimals, number of responses (always 1--this is for compatability with earlier versions of OSIRIS), two missing data codes and a reference number. Note that the starting position, LOCation, is counted from the first column of the first card; for example, V33, Washington Post, which is in column 46 on the second card has LOC 126, 80 (for the first card) + 46.

4.3 Data in OSIRIS

Only numeric variables are suitable for OSIRIS analysis programs. If one is doing analysis it would make no sense to obtain a mean with non-numeric codes. If, on the other hand, one has data which contain non-numeric codes in numeric variables, OSIRIS has provisions for changing them. (Sometimes data have, for example, the coding scheme 0-9, -, &. Ampersands and dashes are occasionlly used when people wish to add code categories to a one digit variable without making it a two column variable. Occasionally one sees sex coded M and F or other alphabetical codings. Although, as indicated, such codes can be fixed in OSIRIS (see section 4.8) it is better to limit a coding scheme to numeric digits. In OSIRIS, if a

38

OUTPUT DICTIONARY

VAR#	VARIABLE NAME	GROUP	COL	WIDTH	NDEC	TYPE	MDCODE1	MDCODE2	RESP	REFNO	ID
V1	STATE	Q1	0	7	2	0	C			1	1
V2	RESPONDENT ID	Q2	0	10	2	0	C			1	2
V3	NUMBER OF CALLS	Q22	0	9	1	0	C	0		1	3
V4	SEX	Q23	0	12	1	0	C			1	4
V5	RACE	Q24	0	13	1	0	C	0		1	5
V6	MARITAL STATUS	Q4	0	14	1	0	C	0		1	6
V7	AGE	Q3	0	15	2	0	C	99		1	7
V8	EDUCATION	Q5	0	17	1	0	A	0		1	8
V9	OCCUPATION	Q7	0	18	2	0	C	0		1	9
V10	EMPLOYMENT STATUS	Q6	0	20	1	0	C	0		1	10
V11	FATHER S OCCUPATION	09	0	22	1	0	C	0		1	11
V12	HUSBAND S OCC	Q8	0	23	2	0	C	0		1	12
V13	CHILDREN IN COLLEGE	Q12	0	25	1	0	C	0		1	13
V14	WORK FOR POL PARTY	Q13	0	26	1	0	C	0		1	14
V15	STUDENT VOICE	Q14	0	27	1	0	C	0		1	15
V16	CONSPIRACY	Q15	0	28	1	0	C	0		1	16
V17	BAN SDS	Q16	0	29	1	0	C	0		1	17
V18	VIET NAM	Q17	0	30	1	0	C	0		1	18
V19	LOT OF AVERAGE MAN	Q18	0	31	1	0	C	0		1	19
V20	CHILD INTO WORLD	Q19	0	32	1	0	C	0		1	20
V21	COUNT ON PEOPLE	Q20	0	33	1	0	C	0		1	21
V22	LIVE FOR TODAY	Q21	0	34	1	0	C	0		1	22
V23	NEAREST LARGE CITY	Q25	0	92	20	0	A	0		1	23
V24	R S COMMUNITY SIZE	Q27	0	21	1	0	C	0		1	24
V25	DIST FROM CITY	Q26	0	112	3	0	C	999		1	25
V26	TRAVEL TIME TO CITY	Q10	0	115	3	1	C	999		1	26

Fig. 4.2 Partial Listing of Campus Unrest
Output Dictionary Created by &DICT

39

variable has non-numeric values, it must be defined initially as an alphabetic variable because in OSIRIS only alphabetic variables may have non-
numeric values. If it is a variable like an address which will always be
used as an alphabetic variable it should remain alphabetic. If it is a
variable containing say, '&'s and '-'s, it should be changed to a numeric
<u>type</u> of variable at the same time the '&'s and '-'s are changed to numbers.

There are two special sorts of non-numeric characters to watch out for.
The first is a complete field of blanks, e.g., a single blank in a variable
with width 1, two adjoining blanks in a variable with width 2, etc. The
second is an embedded blank, e.g., '4ƀ3,', '35ƀ0', or '2ƀ'. All blank
fields and embedded blanks are considered errors when they are found in a
numeric field. OSIRIS has the facilities to repair such variables or to
treat them as missing data. (If an all blank field was meant to stand for
a legitimate code of zero, one would repair the variable; on the other hand
embedded blanks are likely to be errors and often best treated as missing
data.) But since repair takes time and trouble, it is simplest not to use a
blank field as a legitimate code in the first place. Leading blanks, that
is blanks to the left of the most significant digit, are no problem in
OSIRIS. Thus 'ƀ9' and '09' are equivalent and legitimate as are 'ƀƀƀ0' and
'0000'.

OSIRIS data may either have decimal points explicitly punched or implied
(e.g. 1.93 or 193 with two implied decimal places). In either case the
number of decimal places within each variable is recorded in the dictionary. The format of each variable is adjusted when the variable is
referenced.

Negative values in OSIRIS are expressed by a minus sign. Any of the
following are allowable: '-ƀ3', 'ƀ-3', '-03'. On the other hand, '0-3' is
not permitted. Plus signs may be expressed or not.

4.4 Using the &DICT Command

We turn now to the actual mechanics of creating a dictionary. The &DICT
command uses special statements, called variable descriptor statements, to
build the dictionary. Within the &DICT setup, variable descriptor statements follow the parameter card. The parameter card indicates the user's
choice of options for the run such as information to appear on the printed
output and the number of input cards per case. A setup for &DICT using the
Campus Unrest dataset follows.

```
$CREATE MYDICT
$RUN ISR:OSIRIS.IV
&DICT DICTOUT=MYDICT
DICTIONARY FOR CAMPUS UNREST DATA        Label
NREC=2 PRINT=(DI,OUTD)                    Parameter Statement
V=1 NAME='STATE     Q1' WID=2 -           Variable Descriptor
COL=7 RECO=1                              Statements - one
 .                                        statement for each
 .                                        variable the user
 .                                        wants defined
&END
```

There must be one variable descriptor statement for each variable to be
included. Each statement contains information about the location of the
variable on the input data file as well as information about special

characteristics of the variable such as the number of implicit or explicit decimal places, whether it is an alphabetic variable, and the variable's missing data codes. The &DICT command reads these variable descriptor statements and sets up the dictionary with a separate record for each variable using the information from the variable descriptor statements. This dictionary is written to a separate file, the file that was assigned to DICTOUT.

The information about the variables is given using keywords. The keywords for a given variable descriptor statement may be given in any order. They must be separated from each other by one or more blanks or by a comma. Values are assigned to keywords as indicated in Figure 4.3. For example, V= is used to assign a variable number, and COL= is used to indicate the starting column location of the variable.

The variable number and name are transferred to the output dictionary. The variable numbers are used to access variables in later runs. Names are often mnemonics and are printed when the variable is accessed by an OSIRIS program. When a study contains a large number of variables, it is sometimes difficult to distinguish different names in the 24 characters allowed. The original question number is often included as part of the name to ensure later comprehensibility. In addition some standard abbreviations may be used.[9]

One snare in the specification of variable location is that record numbers (RECO=)do not refer to the deck ID constants but rather to the sequential position of the deck relative to other decks. For example, the Campus Unrest Data contain two data decks (two records) per case that are distinguished by the deck ID constants 10 and 12; on variable descriptor statements they are referred to as 1 and 2, their sequential positions.

NDEC and TY indicate special characteristics of the variable. NDEC indicates the number of decimal places in the variable. TY indicates the type of the variable, normally C, for character numeric. Other type code possibilities (there are seven altogether) include A for alphabetic and F for floating-point binary.

```
V=1  NAME='STATE              Q1'   WID=2 COL=7 RECO=1
V=2  NAME='RESPONDENT ID       Q2'   WID=2 COL=10
V=3  NAME='NUMBER OF CALLS     Q22'  WID=1 COL=9 MD1=0
V=4  NAME='SEX                 Q23'  WID=1 COL=12 MD1=NONE
```

Fig. 4.3. Four Sample Variable Descriptor Statements

A description of missing data was presented in Chapter 2. Missing data codes for each variable are defined on the variable descriptor statements. These codes are transferred to the output dictionary. When an OSIRIS analysis program checks for missing data, the value of the variable for each case is checked against its missing data codes as defined in the dictionary and the case is excluded if a match is found. Two missing data codes can be specified. The first missing data code signals as missing any data value equal to the code specified; the second missing data code sig-

---

[9]The Inter-University Consortium for Political and Social Research has a set of such standards. The COL=, RECO=, and WID=, keywords, which refer to the column number, record number (e.g., card deck), and width of the variable, locate the variable in the data file.

nals as missing any data value equal to or greater than the specified code (or equal to or less than if the specified code is negative). A one column coding scheme commonly used is:

```
0.  inappropriate
1.  yes
5.  no
8.  don't know
9.  not ascertained
```

The only codes with substantive information are 1 and 5. On such a variable MD1 could be set to 0 with MD2=8. In this way, any data value equal to 0 or greater than or equal to 8 becomes missing data. Missing data values are excluded from many analysis programs; in the above example only cases with codes of 1 and 5 would enter the analysis.

Do not get the two missing data codes confused. A grievous error is setting the MD2 code to 0 rather than the MD1. In this situation any code greater than or equal to 0 is considered to be missing data. No matter how bad your data are--they are rarely that bad.

These missing data codes are, of course, optional. Every variable need not have missing data codes. A variable may have two, one or no missing data codes. These codes exist for the convenience of the user.

A reference number, which may be set using the keyword REF=, is an additional number which may be used to identify a variable. If not specified, &DICT, by default, inserts the variable number in this field. Sometimes, in later data management processes, variables get renumbered; the original variable number however remains in this field and provides a valuable cross reference.

If one is describing many variables which share similar characteristics the keyword defaults eleminate a great deal of specification. For example, if one has a series of three column variables with an implicit decimal place, one need specify only the card, column, width and number of decimals of the initial variable. If this information is not specified on subsequent variables their values and location will be determined from those of the first. That is, the program will calculate the starting location of subsequent variables as being the next available input location after the previous variable. Fig. 4.4 shows some variable descriptor statements which utilize this default system.

```
V=11 NAME='RENT PER ROOM' REC=2 COL=5 ND=2 MD2=99.00 WID=4
V=12 NAME='ELECTRIC BILL'
V=13 NAME='HEATING PER MONTH'
V=14 NAME='OTHER UTILITIES'
V=15 NAME='AGE' WIDTH=2 ND=0 MD1=00 MD2=NONE
```

Fig. 4.4. Variable Descriptor Statements Using Defaults

Variables 12 through 14 are each four columns wide, with two decimal places and a second missing data code of "99.00". Because nothing except a variable number name was specified for these variables the previous definitions apply to them. Notice that when we encounter a variable with a different format it is necessary to reset the inappropriate defaults. For variable 15, if we had not reset the number of decimal places to "0" the previous definition "ND=2" would have been carried over and applied to

42

variable 15. This requirement, of respecifying the initial default, e.g., ND=0, after it has been changed, is the nemesis of &DICT.

4.5 Special Features of &DICT

There are operational characteristics of &DICT that can best be explained by looking at an actual set of variable descriptor statements. Our Campus Unrest variable descriptor statements are given in Figure 4.5; important aspects are circled.

```
V=1  NAME='STATE                  Q1'   WID=2 COL=7 RECO=1
V=2  NAME='RESPONDENT ID          Q2'         COL=10
V=3  NAME='NUMBER OF CALLS        Q22'  WID=1 COL=9 MD1=0
V=4  NAME='SEX                    Q23'        COL=12 MD1=NONE
V=5  NAME='RACE                   Q24'  MD1=0
V=6  NAME='MARTIAL STATUS         Q4'
V=7  NAME='AGE                    Q3'   WID=2 MD1=99
V=8  NAME='EDUCATION              Q5'   WID=1 MD1=0 TY=A
V=9  NAME='OCCUPATION             Q7'   WID=2 TY=C
V=10 NAME='EMPLOYMENT STATUS      Q6'   WID=1
V=11 NAME='FATHER'S OCCUPATION    Q9'         COL=22
V=12 NAME='HUSBAND'S OCCUPATION   Q8'   WID=2
V=13 NAME='CHILDREN IN COLLEGE    Q12'  WID=1
V=14 NAME='WORK FOR POL PARTY     Q13'
V=15 NAME='STUDENT VOICE          Q14'
V=16 NAME='CONSPIRACY             Q15'
V=17 NAME='BAN SDS                Q16'
V=18 NAME='VIET NAM               Q17'
V=19 NAME='LOT OF AVERAGE MAN     Q18'  L='0=MD, 1=DISAGREE, 2=AGREE'
V=20 NAME='CHILD INTO WORLD       Q19'
V=21 NAME='COUNT ON PEOPLE        Q20'
V=22 NAME='LIVE FOR TODAY         Q21'
V=23 NAME='NEAREST BIG CITY       Q25'  WID=20 TY=A COL=12 RECO=2 L=NONE
V=24 NAME='R'S COMMUNITY SIZE     Q27'  WID=1 MD1=0 COL=21 RECO=1 TY=C
V=25 NAME='DIST FROM CITY         Q26'  WID=3 MD1=99 COL=32 RECO= V=26
V=26 NAME='TRAVEL TIME TO CITY    Q10'  ND=1 MD1=99.0
V=27 NAME='NEW YORK TIMES         Q11'  WID=1 MD1=9 COL=40 ND=0
V=28 NAME='ANN ARBOR NEWS         Q11'
V=29 NAME='DETROIT FREE PRESS     011'
V=30 NAME='WALL STREET JOURNAL    Q11'
V=31 NAME='CHRISTIAN SCIENCE MO   Q11'
V=32 NAME='DAILY WORKER           Q11'
V=33 NAME='WASHINGTON POST        Q11'
```

Fig. 4.5. Sample Variable Descriptor Statements

Variable 1: Our variable descriptor statements have the original question number incorporated into the variable name. This is a convenient way to link variable numbers to the original questionnaire. Some reseachers retain the deck number and card column of the original data within the name, e. g. , RESPONDENT ID 1:10-11.

Variable 3: The input location for variable 3 is column 9 on the first deck. This illustrates that the input locations accessed from one card need not be in order. Data may be assembled in any order and even repeated.

43

Variable 8: The code book has the following coding scheme for education.

Q5 Education

0.	Missing data	6.	9 grades
1.	0-4 grades	7.	10 grades
2.	5 grades	8.	11 grades
3.	6 grades	9.	12 grades
4.	7 grades	&.	13-15 grades
5.	8 grades	-.	16 or more (college degree)

We have non-numeric characters in this variable. This means that we must declare the variable alphabetic. (In a separate, later, step we will change the '&'s to '10's, the '-'s to '11's, the width of the variable to 2, and the type to character. But in order to be able to access this variable at all we must start by declaring it alphabetic).

Variable 9: The TYPE keyword defaults to TYPE=C for the first statement. But once it has been changed it defaults to previous statement, so here we must turn it back to 'C'.

Variable 19: Note that code labels may be assigned. These labels apply to subsequent variables until new labels are assigned or until L=NONE is specified.

Variable 26: The important aspect of Variable 26 is its missing data code. We indicated by ND=1 the existence of one decimal point; this decimal point must appear in the missing data value, regardless of whether it is implicit or explicit in the data file.

Variable 27: ND=0 for the first variable descriptor statement. But once number of decimals has been changed ND= defaults to the previous value. Here we reset it to 0.

4.6 Other Uses of &DICT

In the discussion above, &DICT was used to create an initial dictionary; alternatively, &DICT can be used to correct existing dictionaries or to add variables to them. In these later applications an existing dictionary is input to &DICT (DICTIN= old dictionary) as well as a setup including variable descriptor statements. In this way a relatively few variable descriptor statements may be used to make corrections and additions to an old dictionary. For example, one might input to &DICT a dictionary with 400 variables and a setup including 6 variable descriptor statements, 4 for corrections plus 2 additions. The output would be a dictionary with 402 variables. It is not,however, necessary to include all input variables in the output dictionary; by using run the VARS= keyword in the &DICT run the user can specify a subset of variables for the new dictionary. Care should be taken that the new dictionary accurately describes the data for which it is intended.

4.7 Optimizing the Data File

Once the dictionary is built, the dataset may be used by any OSIRIS command. Often, however, it is sensible to reformat the data so that only the variables that are defined in the dictionary appear in the data (which saves storage space on tape or disk). Also the data can be reordered so

44

that it appears in the same order as it does in the dictionary (which is convenient for the researcher). In our Campus Unrest data, for example, each reformatted case would require only 62 bytes of disk storage (the length of the data record described by the dictionary) rather than the 160 bytes (2 x 80) required by the two card images). The &TRANS program is used for such reformatting. After &TRANS, Campus Unrest cases would have the format shown in Figure 4.6.

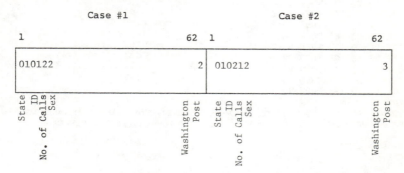

Fig. 4.6. Format of Output Data File Created by &TRANS

&TRANS also produces a revised dictionary, indicating, for example, that Washington Post is in location 62 rather than in location 126. The &TRANS command can also be used to change the storage mode of variables from character to a more efficient mode such as integer or floating point binary mode. The advantage of storing variables in integer or floating point is that OSIRIS analysis runs are then somewhat cheaper; the disadvantage is that integer or floating point variables must be reconverted to character numeric (again using &TRANS) before they can be used outside OSIRIS--say by the MIDAS [7] or SPSS [13], [14] systems.

4.8 Correcting Non-Numeric Characters

The &RECODE command will be described in detail in Chapter 6. It is a powerful command for transforming variables and has many applications. In this section only one minor use will be noted: &RECODE is the command to use in order to correct alphabetic characters in a variable which should be numeric. Consider, for example, V8 in the Campus Unrest Data: because we had two alphabetic codes, '&' and '-', which represent two different levels of schooling, we defined V8 as alphabetic in the dictionary. We can now use &RECODE to change the &'s to 10's and the -'s to 11's. &RECODE normally does temporary recoding only, i.e., the variable transformations made by &RECODE last only for a particular command. However, by using &RECODE in conjunction with &TRANS, a command whose business it is to make a new dataset, one can permanently recode variables. The following setup corrects the amps and dashes in Variable 8 of the Campus Unrest dataset.

The statements (in this instance, twelve tests) that follow the &RECODE are stored away for future reference. The &TRANS command is then invoked. Following the label card is the parameter card: R=1 indicates that each case should be passed to the recode statements before being passed to

45

```
$CREATE NEWDICT
$CREATE NEWDATA
$RUN ISR:OSIRIS.IV
&RECODE
   IF V8 EQ '0' THEN V8=0
   IF V8 EQ '1' THEN V8=1
   IF V8 EQ '2' THEN V8=2
   IF V8 EQ '3' THEN V8=3
   IF V8 EQ '4' THEN V8=4
   IF V8 EQ '5' THEN V8=5
   IF V8 EQ '6' THEN V8=6
   IF V8 EQ '7' THEN V8=7
   IF V8 EQ '8' THEN V8=8
   IF V8 EQ '9' THEN V8=9
   IF V8 EQ '&' THEN V8=10
   IF V8 EQ '-' THEN V8=11
&END
&TRANS DICTIN=MYDICT DICTOUT=NEWDICT DATAIN=CUMERGED DATAOUT=NEWDATA
RECODE AMPS AND DASHES. REFORMAT TO ONE LOGICAL RECORD PER CASE.
R=1 V=1-33
V=8 WID=2 TY=C
&END
```

&TRANS. V=1-33 indicates that variables 1-33 (i.e., all of them) are to be transferred to the new dataset. The next card indicates a dictionary change: in the new dataset V8 should have a width of 2 and be of character type. All the other variables will have their old dictionary information copied to the new dictionary. In this example &TRANS has been used to change a dictionary and, in conjunction &RECODE, to make a permanent copy of corrected data.

Other methods of correcting non-numeric codes are outlined in the Special Techniques section of the "Data Management" chapter in the OSIRIS IV Manual [10]. The second technique under "correcting non-numeric codes in numeric variables" (where A and B are to be recoded to different values) is an alternative to the one given above.

4.9   Using Data Described by an OSIRIS Dictionary

Once data have been described by an OSIRIS dictionary, data fields or variables can be referred to by their variable numbers. Since each variable has a unique variable number, the computer can retrieve all information stored in the dictionary for a variable using the number as an index. Thus the user does not need to keep manually submitting information to the computer about the variables such as where their values start within a data record, their missing data codes, etc., each time the data are used. All this information, which is in machine readable form in the dictionary, can be retrieved by the computer. The user need only tell the computer the name of the dictionary file and the variable numbers of the variable being used. Variables are specified in OSIRIS by either giving the number (261) or preceding the variable number with a V (V261). V261 means the variable with variable number 261.

4.10   Standard OSIRIS Control Statements

Before continuing to use OSIRIS datasets with other programs in the OSIRIS package, a few standard features need to be described.

There are three standard types of control statements used by OSIRIS programs which appear in nearly every setup. These are (i) the filter statements for selecting which cases are to be used, (ii) the label statement for giving a title or label to the printed output from a job, (iii) the parameter statement for selecting the choice of options required for a particular run of a program and for selecting which variables from each case are to be used. These three standard types are described in more detail below.

Some commands require additional special statements; special statements are described in connection with the particular commands which require them. In the OSIRIS manual any special statement is described in the command writeup.

4.11   Filter Statements

Although all the data for a study may be stored in one file, it is often required to perform analysis or data management processes on a subset of the cases in a study. One might for instance have data cases from an entire national sample but for a particular piece of reseach only require cases from one state; or one might want to perform some analyses separately for men and women. The OSIRIS filter is designed to select the cases to be used in a particular run of an OSIRIS program. One selects cases by specifying inclusion or exclusion of cases that satisfy certain conditions. These conditions are given by specifying the variable number of the variable (such as state or sex) on the basis of which selection is to be made and giving the values of that variable which define the cases to be included or excluded. Thus if V4 is the sex variable where a value of 1 means male and 2 means female, then a filter statement 'INCLUDE V4=1' says include only cases where the value of variable 4 equals 1, i.e., include only males. A statement 'EXCLUDE V4=1' says, exclude all cases where variable 4 takes the value of 1, i.e., exclude all males. More complex conditions for selection can be done using AND's and OR's in the filter statement. For example, to select only males over 50 years old, one could use the statement 'INCLUDE V4=1 AND V7=51-98'.

A filter statement must start with either INCLUDE or EXCLUDE. Conditions are expressed by specifying a variable number and the values or ranges of values that are to be allowed. Different expressions may be connected by AND's or OR's. Up to 100 expressions are allowed in one filter statement. A filter may be continued to another line (or card) by placing a dash after the last character in the statement to be continued. More details on the filter statement can be found in the OSIRIS IV Manual [10].

4.12   Label Statements

The label statement may contain any information the user likes and may be up to 100 characters long. (If using cards, put a dash after last character of the first card if you want to continue on to a second card). A label statement must be supplied with most OSIRIS commands. It is used to title the printed output. In nearly all OSIRIS programs, it is the first thing that is printed. In some programs, the label is reprinted at the top of each page of the output.

4.13 Parameter Statements

Most OSIRIS programs, being general purpose, have a variety of different options that can be selected by the user at the time they are used. These options are specified on the parameter statement. Different options are available for different programs and the user must always refer to the writeup for the particular program being used for the options that are available for that program. The options or parameters are specified using keywords, or keywords set equal to values. For example, an option to stop execution of a program after 20 cases with errors have been encountered might be expressed 'MAXERR=20' or an option to write an output file might be expressed with a single keyword 'WRITE'. If a particular keyword is not specified by the user, or a value is not given then the program will assume a 'default' value. The default is what is assumed if the user does not specify something. Defaults are set to give the most commonly used option and it is therefore often not necessary to specify any parameters. The rules for typing (or punching) parameters are that each new option be separated from the last by a comma or any number of blanks; that when a keyword has more than four characters, only the first four (sometimes less) need be specified; that any number of lines may be used (or cards); that to continue a parameter statement on to a new line (or card) a dash should be placed after the last character of the line to be continued (if between keywords, put a space, then the dash). It should be noted that if all default options are chosen, a blank parameter card or one containing an asterisk must still be supplied (if at a terminal, give a blank line or an asterisk).

An example of a parameter statement that might be used with the &DICT program is:

    NRECORDS=3 PRINT=DICT

This card could equally well be spread onto two cards:

    NRECORDS=3 -

    PRINT=DICT

Or punched with only four characters per keyword:

    NREC=3 PRIN=DICT

Or punched with still further abbreviation (discovered by consulting the writeup for the command in the OSIRIS Manual):

    NREC=3 P=DI

When a data file is being accessed, usually only a few variables from each case are required for a particular process. Typically, the variables required are selected by using a VARS= keyword on the parameter statement. Following the = is a list of variables. Variables are referenced by specifying their variable number (optionally preceded by a V, e.g., V261). These are sometimes called V-type variables and are always described in a dictionary. It will be seen in Chapter 6 that there is a feature in OSIRIS whereby new variables can constructed for the duration of one analysis. Such new variables are called result, or R-type, variables. These are referenced by preceding the result number with an R, e.g., R2. A variable list is a list of variables (V-type and/or R-type) specified as single variables or ranges, with commas separating the items. An example VARS= keyword with a list is VARS= V6, V9-V12, R3, V7.

The difference between the filter and the VARS= keyword is that the filter identifies which <u>cases</u> are to be accessed; having selected the cases, the VARS= variable list identifies which <u>variables</u> from each of those cases are required.

Succeeding chapters show examples of the use of OSIRIS datasets and these different kinds of control statements with both data management and analysis programs in the OSIRIS package.

Chapter 5

DATA CLEANING AND DATA MANAGEMENT

5.1 Checking for Coding Errors

Wild Code Checking

Each variable in the data has a list of permissible values or codes as
specified in the code book. Values not in this list are known as _wild_
codes. Alphabetic values in numeric variables are one kind of wild code.
Reporting of wild codes is the function of the OSIRIS wild code check command (&WCC). This program reads through a data file and checks for wild
codes according to user specifications of the valid codes for particular
variables. These valid code specifications are specified at the time the
wild code check program is run. If no code specification is given the command simply checks for nonnumeric values.

Each time a wild, or illegitimate code is encountered, the program
prints identification information for the case in error, together with the
relevant variable numbers and their offending values. One can then return
to the interview and coding sheets for say, interview number 943 and determine why it has a value of "6" on variable 7 when only codes 0, 1, 5, and 9
are listed in the codebook.

An example of a setup for checking for wild codes in the Campus Unrest
data is given below.

```
$RUN ISR:OSIRIS.IV
&WCC DICTIN=NEWDICT DATAIN=NEWDATA
CHECK WILD CODES
ID=(1,2,23)
V=3,5,6,18 MIN=0 MAX=3
V=4 CODES=1-2
V=12 MIN=0 MAX=14
V=17 CODES=0-2
V=1-2,7-11,13-16,19-33
&END
```

This run of &WCC checks wild numeric codes in selected variables and
checks nonnumeric codes for all numeric variables. On the parameter statement (see ID= keyword) are given the variable numbers of the variables
whose values are to be listed when a case with wild codes is encountered;
identification variables should be specified (for the Campus Unrest data,
variables 1 and 2) and any others of particular interest (in this example
variable 23 is also printed). The first four code specification statements
check for valid codes on variables 3-6, 12 and 17-18. MIN= and MAX= values
can often be used instead of the CODES= keyword and are preferable because
they reduce execution time. The first specification could read CODES=0-3
but that would not be as efficient. The fifth code specification statement
checks the remaining numeric variables for alphabetics.

It is not necessary to check for numeric wild codes on every variable.
Instead, one can first establish which variables have wild codes and then
use the wild code program to identify the actual cases where those variables are in error. The presence or absence of any numeric wild codes can
be detected from marginal distributions for each variable. Marginals con-

51

sist of a count of the number of cases falling in each code category for a variable. If one gets non-zero counts for a particular variable in code categories which are not in the code book, the variable has wild codes. The marginals do not give which cases are in error, however, but only that in some cases, a variable has a wild code. Thus, only those variables which have non-zero marginals in incorrect code categories need be checked by the wild code check program. The wild code check program will list which cases contain the wild codes in those variables. Marginal distributions can be produced by the OSIRIS &TABLES command which is discussed in Chapter 7.

Consistency Checking

The values of some variables may depend on the values of other variables. For example, one doesn't ask a man what his husband's occupation is. In other words if the respondent is coded as a male on the sex variable, then his value for the husband's occupation variable should be the inapplicable code. If this is not the case, then the values of the two variables sex and husband's occupation are inconsistent. Another kind of consistency check looks for unlikely combinations of characteristics, such as a doctor with no college education.

The &CONCHECK command can be used to detect such inconsistencies. &CONCHECK is always used in conjunction with the &RECODE command which is described fully in Chapter 6. The consistency check conditions are expressed in &RECODE. The variables to be printed if an inconsistency is discovered are specified in the &CONCHECK setup. The following example checks for two inconsistencies:

(i) If age (V7) is less than 18, then occupation (V9) should be student.

(ii) Husband's occupation (V12) is inapplicable for single people (V6=2) and for men (V4=1).

```
$RUN ISR:OSIRIS.IV
&RECODE
   IF V7 LT 18 AND V9 NE 10 THEN R100=1 ELSE R100=0
   IF (V4 EQ 1 OR V6 EQ 2) AND V12 NE 0 THEN R101=1 ELSE R101=0
&END
&CONCHECK DICTIN=NEWDICT DATAIN=NEWDATA
PERFORMING CONSISTENCY CHECKS
RECODE=1 ID=(IDVARS=1-2)
R100=1 V=7,9,R100 NAME='OCC SHOULD BE STUDENT'
R101=1 V=4,6,12,R101 NAME='HUSBANDS OCC SHOULD BE INAP'
&END
```

The ID= keyword on &CONCHECK parameter card is used to specify identification variables which should be printed whatever the error. The Rn= keywords on the condition statements each specify a result number for a particular consistency test and a value which signals an inconsistency for the test. In this example, results are set to 1 if inconsistencies are found. The V= keywords on the condition statements specify the particular variables which should be printed whenever there is an inconsistency.

5.2 Correcting Data Files

Coding errors and totally invalid cases have now been detected at three separate stages: (i) from the merge checking when cases with missing, bad or duplicate decks were reported (ii) from wild code checking and (iii) from consistency checks. The appropriate correct values for the faulty cases and variables must be found by going back to the original questionnaires. Once this has been done, the data file can be corrected.

The general procedure for correcting fields on a disk or tape file is shown diagrammaticaly in Fig. 5.1. A record is read from the original file into the memory by a correction program. If a correction is required (as indicated by a correction statement for the same respondent) then the appropriate fields are changed in the memory and the record is then written out to the disk or tape containing the corrected data file. The process continues for each input record in turn. At the end of the process, the original file still exists and in addition we have a corrected file. It is important to notice that in OSIRIS it is not possible to update fields directly on the original disk or tape just as it would be impossible on a conventional tape recorder to change one word or sentence without destroying other words or sentences. Updating disks or tapes in OSIRIS always involves reading from one disk or tape and writing to another.

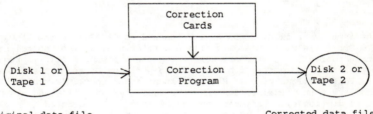

Original data file   Corrected data file

Fig. 5.1 Procedure for Correcting Fields on a Disk or Tape File
(The input and output dictionaries are not shown in this diagram; the output dictionary is simply a copy of the input dictionary.)

The command in OSIRIS for correcting data files (which may be on disk or tape) is called &FCOR (file correct). The user must specify the variable numbers of the variables that will be used to identify the cases to be corrected. These are the ID variables. Correction statements are then supplied that give the appropriate values of the ID variables and specify the variables that are to be changed along with the new values that they are to take.

An example is given below.

53

```
$CREATE DI4
$CREATE DA4
$RUN ISR:OSIRIS.IV
&FCOR DICTIN=NEWDICT DATAIN=NEWDATA DICTOUT=DI4 DATAOUT=DA4
RUN TO MAKE CORRECTIONS ON CAMPUS UNREST DATA          Label
ID=1,2                                                 Parameter Stmt.
ID=(1,7) V4=1, V12=0
ID=(2,1) V12=0
ID=(2,10) V11=1                                        Instruction
ID=(2,11) ADD V3=1, V4=2, V5=1, V6=3, V7=23, V8=9, V9=25 - Statements
V10=2, V11=7, V12=0, V13=1, V14=1, V15=1, V16=1, V17=1,-
V18=1, V19=1, V20=1, V21=2, V22=1, V23=MESA, V24=5, -
V25=017, V26=.5, V27=1, V28=2, V29=3, V30=3, V31=3, V32=9 -
V33=9
ID=(3,5) V23=FRESNO, V25=000, V26=000, V27=3, V28=9, V29=9, V30=3 -
V31=3, V32=3, V33=3
ID=(4,7) V5=1, V6=0
ID=(4,11) DEL
ID=(5,4) V18=3, V17=2
ID=(5,9) V3=1, V4=1, V5=1, V6=2, V7=47, V8=9, V9=4, V10=1, V11=4, -
V12=0, V13=3, V14=1, V15=2, V16=2, V17=1, V18=1, V19=2 -
V20=1, V21=2, V22=1, V24=4, V25=999, V26=99.9
ID=(23,56) DEL
ID=(99,99) DEL
&END
```

The input data file, NEWDATA, is attached to DATAIN= on the &FCOR command. Since fields in the data file are referenced in the control cards by variable numbers, a dictionary describing the input data file is required that will tell the correction command the position of the variables in the data. This dictionary, here NEWDICT, is attached to DICTIN. DICTOUT and DATAOUT are then needed to describe the corrected data file and its associated dictionary. Variables cannot be added to or deleted from records, nor can the field widths of variables can be changed by this program. The only function the program has with respect to variables is to change values of existing variables within a record.

The ID= keyword on the parameter statement for the &FCOR command specifies which variables are to be used as ID variables. In the Campus Unrest data, each case requires two variables for unique identification--a State ID and Respondent ID within that State. The instruction statements give the values for the ID variables for the cases to be corrected along with the new values of variables that are to be changed.

It is important that the data records on the input file are sorted into the same order as the instruction statements. The program works by reading the first instruction statement, reading data records and copying them to the output file until a match with the instruction statement is found, making the correction, reading the next instruction statement and continuing reading and copying the input file until the next match is found and so on. If the corrections were not ordered in the same way as the input file, matches would never be found. Normally data files are kept sorted in order by the identification variables, and instruction statements are likewise ordered.

[The following detail is of particular interest to readers who are processing the Campus Unrest data. If the reader has been following the sample setups and printouts in Appendices B and C, he will have noted a

problem with state 05, respondent 9. After the &MERCHECK run, two complete
cases exist, one with state code ð5 and the other with state code 05.
&FCOR, however, treats blanks and zeroes as equivalent. In order for &FCOR
to work the offending case must be removed before &FCOR processes it. It
should be deleted by a filter in the &FCOR run - see the &FCOR setup in Appendix B. The reason that &FCOR won't work if it "sees" the 05 case is that
&FCOR requires that the input data be sorted on the identification variables. After &MERCHECK the cases are in the following order: 5 9; 510; 05
9. To &FCOR, which treats 5 and 05 as equivalent, these cases are out of
order.]

There are two additional functions of the &FCOR command that have to do
with cases. The first is to delete complete input cases. This can be
achieved by delete keyword which can be specified for a particular case ID
in place of the normal correction card format. The second is to add cases
by specifying the ID, the keyword ADD, and variable numbers with associated
values.

5.3 Listing Data Values From a File

One important facility necessary when using data stored on a machine
readable medium (cards, tape, disk) is to be able to make a printed listing
of the data. Every computer installation will have some kind of simple
utility program for doing this job, often supplied by the manufacturer.
MTS, for example, has a command $LIST while IBM supplies a utility IEBPTPCH
for all OS installations of the IBM 360/370 computer. Such programs
produce listings but are often somewhat inflexible in what they print and
how it is formated on the page.

There is a special listing command in the OSIRIS package, &DSLIST, for
listing the dictionary and data of OSIRIS datasets. With this program, the
user may elect to have all the records in a file listed, or a specified
subset, the data printed as a string of values, or the values for each
variable separated from each other. The user can also elect whether or not
to have the dictionary printed for the variables that were selected.

An example of a setup for using the &DSLIST command to print the data
values for a subset of variables for women over 60, from the Campus Unrest
Data is:

```
$RUN ISR:OSIRIS.IV
&DSLIST DICTIN=DI4 DATAIN=DA4
INCLUDE V4=1 AND V7=61-98        Filter to select women over 60
LISTING DATA VALUES FOR OLDER WOMEN Label
PRINT=DICT V=1-3,5-6,10-12       Parameters to select variables
&END                             and get dictionary printout
                                 for those variables
```

If only a listing of the dictionary is desired, use the CASES keyword on
the parameter statement (set CASES=0). If only a listing of the data
values is desired, omit PRINT=DICT.

5.4 Deleting or Subsetting Variables and Cases From Data Files

Sometimes it is desirable to create a subset of a file either in order to delete unwanted variables and/or cases, or to create a work file from a large file in order to save execution time on runs which do not require the complete data base. Whenever variables are deleted from records, the format of the record is changed. If the record format is described in machine readable form, for example by an OSIRIS dictionary, then a new version of this descriptive information will be required for the subsetted file.

The OSIRIS &TRANS command can be used to subset an OSIRIS dataset by variable or by case or by both. (It can also be used to make an exact copy of an OSIRIS dataset --dictionary and data; alternatively, &COPYSORT can be used to make a copy of a dataset). Subsetting by case is achieved by use of an appropriate filter statement and the subsetting by variable is achieved by supplying a list of the desired variables. The output data file created by &TRANS contains only those cases that passed the filter and each of the cases contains only those variables specified in the variable list. An output dictionary is automatically written which contains only dictionary records for the subset of the variable selected.

An example of a &TRANS run is:

```
$CREATE DICU5
$CREATE DACU5
$RUN ISR:OSIRIS.IV
&TRANS DICTIN=DI4 DATAIN=DA4 DICTOUT=DICU5 DATAOUT=DACU5
INCLUDE V1=1,3                                          Filter
FILE FOR MICH. AND CALIF. WITHOUT ATTITUDE ITEMS       Label
V=1-13,23-33                                            Parameter
&END
```

The OSIRIS &UPDATE command, discussed in section 5.6 in connection with combining datasets, can also be used to subset variables and cases from a single file.

5.5 Adding Variables to Data Records

It is often necessary to add variables to existing data records. Some examples of types of instances where this might occur are:

1. Some questions or variables from a study, by oversight or intention, were not coded or transferred to machine readable form with the rest of the study's data. Later, it is found that these variables are required.

2. Variables from an existing data base or archive are required as additional information in a study about the same respondents. For example, if data are collected about states, it might be desired to add census data or the like from an existing data base.

3. Panel studies usually require the addition of variables collected at one time to the data records containing variables for the same respondents from previous waves of the study.

4. Aggregate data is required attached to each respondent's data.

56

For example, one might want to add variables about a neighborhood to each individual respondent's data record where several respondents live in the same neighborhood.

5. The addition of new variables computed or derived from existing variables in each of the data records in a file. This type of processing will be covered in Chapter 6.

Instances 1-4 above require that data records from one source be matched with data records from another source, and a combined data record constructed containing variables from each. There is always the possibility, however, that there is not a match for a particular record in each of the sources being combined. A decision then has to be made as to what the output file should contain. The four possible approches are illustrated by means of Venn diagrams in Fig.5.2 when two files A and B are being matched.

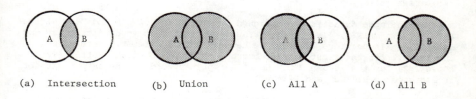

(a) Intersection   (b) Union   (c) All A   (d) All B

Figure. 5.2 Four Approaches to Output File Content

In (a) cases are only selected and merged if there is a match in files A and B (a record with the same identification appears in each file). In (b) the output file will contain one record for every record that occurs either in A or B or both. In (c) the output file will contain one record for every record in A. In (d), the output file will contain one record for every record in B. In cases (b-d) there will be some output records for which information is missing. For example, in (c) there will be some cases which only appeared in the A file. Values for variables from B that are missing in these unmatched cases have to be 'padded' in with some prespecified values.

5.6   OSIRIS &UPDATE Command for Merging Files

Variables from one source may be merged into data records from one or more other sources with the OSIRIS &UPDATE command. This program is designed to accept one or more input OSIRIS datasets and output one new OSIRIS dataset according to user specifications. One of the four methods shown in Fig. 5.2 for selecting which cases are to be part of the output file may be chosen using the OPT= keyword on update statements; filters can be optionally applied to any of the input files; variables to be incorporated may be selected for each file separately. In addition the program has a HOLD option whereby files at different levels of aggregation can be match merged, with variables from the higher level of aggregation being added to several data records at a lower level of aggregation. An example of using this command is given below. Here two input files are being merged.

```
$CREATE DI5
$CREATE DA5
$RUN ISR:OSIRIS.IV
&UPDATE DICTIN=DI4 DATAIN=DA4 DICTIN2=NEWDIC DATAIN2=NEWDAT -
    DICTOUT=DI5  DATAOUT=DA5
ADDING 4 VARIABLES TO CAMPUS UNREST DATASET        Label
PRINT=OUTD                                         Parameter Statement
INFILE=IN ID=1-2 V=1-33                            Update Statements
INFILE=IN2 ID=1-2 V=3-6 RENU=(V3-V6:V34-V37)
&END
```

Four variables from a separate OSIRIS dataset (NEWDIC and NEWDAT) are being added to each record in the Campus Unrest Dataset. Variables 1 and 2 are the State and Person ID respectively on each file, and matching of records from the two files is performed by searching for matches on these two variables.

The two input datasets are assigned to DICTIN and DATAIN and DICTIN2 and DATAIN2. In OSIRIS, 'IN' is the default suffix for an input dictionary and data file. In previous examples we have used this default. Here we use the default for the first dataset but had to supply a unique suffix (we chose IN2) for the second DICT and DATA input keywords. The output dataset is assigned to DICTOUT and DATAOUT.

Turning to the control statements, there are the usual label statement and parameter statement (here printing the output dictionary). The following two statements are Update Statements, one for each input file. The IN-FILE keywords are used to define the input file which is being described. (INFILE=IN is the default and is not necessary but is specified here to help make the setup clear. It is always permissible to specify a default.) The ID= keywords give the matching rules -- i. e. , that variables 1 and 2 in the file with suffix 'IN' must match variables 1 and 2 in the file with suffix 'IN2'.

In this example, by default, the intersection option (see Figure 5.2) has been selected. There is a keyword 'OPT' which can specify for any file that a matching record from that file is not necessary in order to make an output case (a missing data code or zeros, depending on how the keyword PAD= is set, will be used in place of the missing set of variable values). In this example records from neither file are optional: there must be matching records from both files to make an output case. The V= keywords list the variables that are to be included in each output record - all 33 variables from the Campus Unrest data plus four new variables(V3-V6) from the new dataset. The new variables are to be renumbered. Variables 1 and 2 are not selected from the 'IN2' file since they are identical to variables 1 and 2 on the 'IN' file. The final output OSIRIS dataset will consist of a dictionary describing 37 variables plus a data file where each record contains values for 33 variables from the Campus Unrest data plus values for 4 variables from the new dataset. Figure 5.3 shows this process diagrammatically.

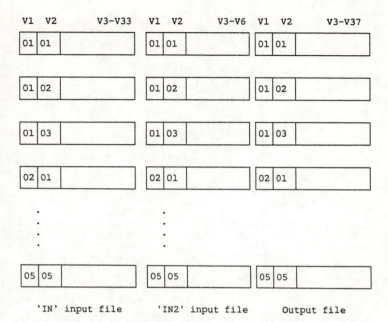

'IN' input file   'IN2' input file   Output file

Fig. 5.3 Merging New Variables into a Data File

The &UPDATE command may be used to process several input files simultaneously, rather than just two as shown above. The output is always a single, updated, file. Input files must be sorted on the identification variables (or use the SORT= keyword on the update statement and supply a file for the sorted data on the command). If the input files are on tape, then each must be on a separate tape (one cannot read two files in parallel from the same tape).

59

Chapter 6

VARIABLE TRANSFORMATION AND DATA REDUCTION

6.1 Reasons for Variable Transformation

Often in the analysis of social science data the analyst is interested
in modifications or transformations of the variables that exist in the data
file being used. For example, the analyst might be interested in the total
income of a respondent where total income is the sum of several variables
(e.g., income from salary, income from property, income from investments,
and other income); or questions may have been asked about the possession of
various items (e.g., television, washing machine, dish washer,
refrigerator)--each resulting in a yes or no answer and the analyst might
be interested only in a single index containing the total number, or count,
of items from the set that the respondent possesses; a third type of transformation might involve the collapsing of values for a continuous variable
such as income into a limited number of discrete categories (e. g. , high,
medium, and low income).

If the new variables are to be used only for a particular analysis and
are not written to a permanent output file the recoding can be 'temporary'.
For preliminary analytical runs, it is advisable to be able to try out new
variables with such temporary recording without going through the extra
work of creating a new data file. Once it has been decided that certain
recoded variables have been created correctly and are going to be needed
frequently, it may be preferable to write a new data file containing the
new variables in a permanent form so that they can be accessed directly for
subsequent runs.

6.2 Logistics of Variable Transformation

In order to create new variables according to the values of variables
existing on an input data file, the rules for constructing the new variables must be specified. A computer program can then read and interpret
these instructions and apply them to the data. The values of the variables
created can then be used directly by a command; alternatively, a new data
record containing values for old and new variables can be written to a new
file.

Figures 6.1 and 6.2 give pictorial representations of the process as it
is performed in OSIRIS. The OSIRIS &RECODE command is always used in conjunction with another command; if it is used in conjunction with &TRANS,
the file creation command, a permanent copy of the new variables may be
created (see top part of Fig. 6.1). As indicated in Figure 6.2, the OSIRIS
recoding instructions are applied to each case immediately after it is
read. Then the new variables, as well as the old variables, for that case
are passed to the waiting program for processing. While such case by case
is the most common method of stepping through the data (see also, for example, SPSS [13], [14], BMDP [2], and SAS [11], [12]), variable by variable
processing is used by some systems (notably, MIDAS [7]).

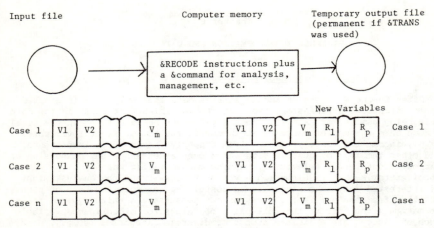

Input file   Computer memory   Temporary output file
                                                   (permanent if &TRANS
                                                   was used)

&RECODE instructions plus
a &command for analysis,
management, etc.

Fig. 6.1. Chart Showing Input and Output in Recoding Process

6.3 Recoding or Variable Transformation With OSIRIS

The usual way recoding is performed in OSIRIS is by the OSIRIS &RECODE command. &RECODE is a programming language in which the user can express requirements for variable creation. The new variables are created in the computer memory as the data cases are read and their values can be passed to the command that is being used. In this case the recoding is temporary--variables are created for the duration of the command only. Permanent versions of new variables can be retained on an output file by use of RECODE in conjunction with the OSIRIS command &TRANS.

As for any language, the recoding language has fixed syntactical rules which the user must follow in order to write his requirements. These syntactical rules and a complete description of the entire language can be found in the OSIRIS IV Manual [10], and no attempt will be made here to repeat this detailed information. Instead, a brief overview of the major components of the language will be presented along with examples of typical usages of some of the features.

A set of recoding instructions is incorporated and used in a run by preparing appropriate statements and placing them in a setup immediately following a &RECODE command as shown in the example below of using recoding with a run of the &TABLES command. The &RECODE command and statements must precede the command that uses them.

```
$RUN ISR:OSIRIS.IV
&RECODE
   Recode statements
&TABLES DICTIN=        DATAIN=
   Control cards for &TABLES
&END
```

The recoding instructions are of two basic kinds:

(i) Initialization statements which set values of missing data codes,
    variable names, and set up recoding tables; initialization state-

62

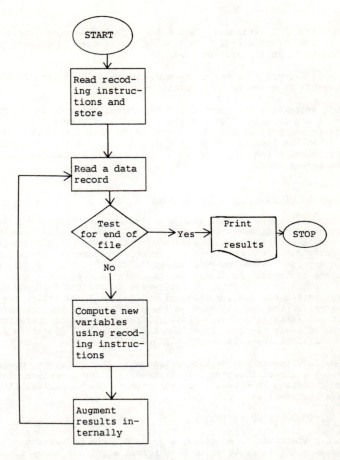

Fig. 6.2. Flowchart of Temporary Recoding Process During a Run

ments are done once, at the beginning of
the run.

(ii) Executable statements which are executed in order upon each data
record passing the filter (if any) before that data record is
used in management or analytical computations.

New variables are created by performing some operation or function on
existing variables (or ones constructed in earlier recode statements) and
placing the result either in a result variable (R-type variable) or by
replacing the values of an existing variable (V-type variable). For example, the statement

R1=V5+V6

adds the values of variables 5 and 6 for a particular case and places the result in new variable --R1. This value may be used in the analysis by referring to R1 in the list of analysis variables.

A simple example of a set of recode statements to create four new variables (R1-R4) is given below in Figure 6.3.

Recode statements are punched in free format starting in column 2. If statements are labelled (for example A and B in Figure 6.3), the label is punched beginning in columns 1 and may not be more than 4 characters long. If more than one line (or card) is needed for a statement put a dash as the last character on the statement to be continued. A statement may be up to 1024 characters long.

6.4 Elements of OSIRIS Recode Language

The basic elements used in recode statements are operands. There are three types of operands--V-type variables, R-type variables and constants. V-type variables are variables existing on the input file being accessed. R-type variables are constructed with recode statements; these can be used as temporary results for computation of further results, or they can be used in the analysis. Constants can be either conventional numeric constants, alphabetic constants, or references to missing data codes of V-type or R-type variables, e.g., MD1(V6) or MD2(R4). (These latter are defined at the start of the run either from the dictionary or through recode missing data initialization statements.) Different kinds of operations may be performed on these operands by arithmetic and logical operators and functions. A list of these is given in Fig.6.4.

The basic elements of the recode language--the operators, operands and functions are linked together into statements. The execution of these statements results in values being assigned to new variables. An example of such a statement is:

R1=SQRT(ABS(V2-R4*10))

When such a statement is executed, a value for the expression on the right is computed and then assigned to R1. Normal algebraic conventions are used in determining the order in which the expression is evaluated. The "V" in front of the variable number is required in recode statements.

The execution of statements can be conditional by using logical operators. For example:

IF V5 EQ 0 THEN R1=0 ELSE R1=BRAC(V6,0-1=1,2-5=2,ELSE=3)

In this example a value of 0 is assigned to R1 if V5 is equal to 0; otherwise a value for R1 is set according to the value of V6. The general form of such a conditional or logical statement is:

IF X THEN Y1 [AND Y2 AND ---] ELSE Z1 [AND Z2 AND ---]

Which says: if expression 'X' is true, then execute the statements Y1, Y2 ---etc. If the expression 'X' is false, then execute the statements Z1, Z2 ---etc. If the 'ELSE' clause is absent, then the next statement is used.

```
R1=BRAC (V19,0-99=1,100-499=2,500-999=3)      Assignment statement
                                              using bracket function

IF V206 GT 9 THEN R2=9 ELSE R2=V206           Logical expression
                                              and 2 alternative
                                              assignments

IF V16 EQ MD1(V16) THEN GO TO A               Logical expression
                                              and branch

R3=V16+V17                                    Arithmetic expression
                                              and assignment

GO TO B                                       Control statement

A R3=V17                                      Labelled assignment
                                              Statement

B R4=RECODE V3,V4,(1/1)=1,(2/2)=2,ELSE=3      Assignment using
                                              Recoding function

NAME R1'BRACKETED INCOME', R2'EDUCATION'      Name initialization
                                              statement

MDATA R4(3)                                   Missing data
                                              initialization
                                              statement
```

Fig. 6.3 Some Sample Recode Statments

Arithmetic Operators

+,-,*,/   addition, subtraction, multiplication, division

Arithmetic Simple Functions

EXP   exponentiation
ABS   absolute value
LOG   logarithm to the base 10
SQRT   square root
TRUNC   truncate to integral part (no rounding)

Logical Operators and Connectors

LT   less than
LE   less than or equal
GT   greater than
GE   greater than or equal
EQ   equal
NE   not equal
AND   and
OR   or
NOT   not

Arithmetic Special Functions

RAND   creates a random number
BRAC   collapses values into categories
TABLE   sets a value according to the values of two variables
COUNT   counts the number of occurrences of a particular
          constant in a set of variables
RECODE   sets a value according to the values of up to 12
          variables
COMBINE   creates one pattern or combination variable from up to
          13 variables
DUMMY   creates dummy variables according to sets of values of
          one variable
SELECT   selects a variable from a list according to an index

Logical Special Functions

MDATA   tests for missing data in a list of up to 50 variables
INLIST   tests for the existence of a variable value in a list of
          constants
EOF   causes recode statements to be executed once more after
          an end of file (used for aggregation)

Fig. 6.4. Operators and Functions in the OSIRIS RECODE

66

Three special types of statements are available, control statements, initialization statements, and one "special" statement. Normally recode statements are executed once per case, one after another. Control statements can be used to alter this normal flow of processing. The most commonly used control statement is a GO TO in conjunction with a label attached to another statement: in this way the order in which the statements are executed can be changed. For example:

```
IF V6 EQ 9 THEN GO TO ABC
R10=V6+V7*(V9*3)
R11=BRAC(V11,0=0,ELSE=1)
ABC IF ----
```

Initialization statements are for setting initial values at the start of a run. They are not executed as data cases are read, but used only once when the dictionary describing the data is read. Initialization statements include:

(i) MDATA   Assigns first or second missing data codes to R or V type variables

              e.g., MDATA R1(9),R2(0,9),R3(,8)

(ii) NAME   Assigns names to R or V type variables

              e.g., NAME R2'CONSUMER INDEX'

(iii) TABLE   Defines the rows and columns of a two way table along with the cell values which will result when a table is is referred to in an arithmetic expression.

              e.g., TABLE 1 COLS 0,1,2,3 ROWS 1(1,1,2,3) - 2(2,3,4,4,) 3(3,3,3,4,5) ENDTAB

(iv) CARRY   Sets values of specified R-variables to 0 at the start of a run; these are then not reinitialized to missing data at the start of each new data case. Can be used in conjunction with the SELECT statement to "break apart" single records into multiple ones.

              e.g., CARRY (R1-R9)

The "special" statement is a RECODE statement, e.g., RECODE=10. A RECODE statement is different from a &RECODE command or the RECODE function! A RECODE statement is used to assign a number to the set of RECODE statements. It may also be used to set the mode of &RECODE. Mode is discussed in section 6.6.

6.5   Handling of Missing Data by OSIRIS Recode

There is no automatic check for missing data embodied in any recode statement. If a variable has a missing data code and this code occurs in some data cases, then these cases must be handled through the use of appropriate recode statements. It makes no sense, for example, to perform an arithmetic computation if one of the operand's values is a missing data code.

Missing data can be checked through use of the MDATA logical function, e.g.:

    IF MDATA(V5, V6,) THEN R1=MD1(R1) ELSE R1=V5+V6

In this example the MDATA function checks for missing data 1 and missing data 2 on the two variables. R1 is set to its first missing data code if either missing data code is found in either variable. Otherwise the computation is performed.

Since the MDATA function checks for both first and second missing data codes, unnecessary instructions are generated and executed by RECODE in the case where a variable only has a first missing data code. In this case it is more economical both for storage space and execution time to code:

    IF V5 EQ MD1(V5) OR V6 EQ MD1 (V6) THEN R1=MD1(R1) ELSE R1=V5+V6

The values of the operands: MD1(Variable number), MD2 (Variable number) are set at the start of the recode process and remain constant throughout the run. The values they take can be set through MDATA statements for the variables. If a V-type variable's missing data codes are not set through an MDATA statement, then values from the dictionary are used. If there are no values specified in the dictionary, then the default values of 1.5^{10} and 1.6^{10} are used, respectively, for MD1 and MD2.

6.6 Handling of Decimal Places by OSIRIS Recode

&RECODE normally operates in floating point mode; this mode will work with all OSIRIS commands. If, however, you are using a command which accepts only integers you may wish to specify integer on the RECODE statement. (Currently &SEARCH, &MNA, &SCAT, and &TABLES are the only integer programs.) This will increase efficiency. But be careful. Not only will any implied decimal places for variables, as given in the dictionary records, be ignored, but, in addition, fractional parts of results of computations caused by recoding statements will be dropped--the result value will merely be truncated to its integral part. Constants may not contain decimal places when using RECODE in integer mode, nor may the LOG or SQRT functions be accessed.

In the normal, floating point, mode of &RECODE operation, data values are used with the correct number of decimal places. Accuracy in this mode is to seven significant digits (1234567. or 1234.567 or .1234567), e.g., the number 6923.40156 could be anything between 6923.40099 and 6923.40199. Large integers are therefore not accurately represented if recoding is being done in floating point. Fractional results of computations are retained. However, since numbers are not recorded exactly, it is possible that when results of recode operations are tested against constants in later steps, equality will never be found. For example, consider the two statements

    R1=V5/V6
    IF (R1 EQ 2) THEN R2=10

R1 may never equal exactly 2 (it may be anywhere between 1.9999999 and 2.00000009) due to the not completely exact recording of the value of R1. One might instead have to substitute a statement

IF R1 GT 1.999 AND R1 LT 2.0001 THEN R2=10

If the same statements are used in integer mode, R1 will always take an integral value (the truncated result of dividing V5 by V6) and it is always possible to compare this for equality to an integer constant.

6.7   How OSIRIS Recode Stores New Values

. Recoding is performed case by case as described in section 6. 2. That is, the input data for one case is read into the memory, each of the specified recode operations is performed in turn, and data from this case used; the next case is then processed. For each of the variables read from the input file and each of the results mentioned in the recode statements, one location is reserved in the memory. When a new variable value is computed it is stored in the location reserved for that variable number. Any value previously existing for that variable is overwritten. Before the start of processing of each case, each R-type variable is automatically initialized to a large number (1.5×10^9) (except R-type variables iniitialized by the CARRY statement). An example of this process is shown in Figure 6.5.

Recode statements:

   R1=BRAC(V6,0=0,1-5=1,ELSE=2)   Statement 1

   V7=BRAC(V7,0-3=1,4-9=2)   Statement 2

   V6=R1 + V7   Statement 3

Data case read contains: V6=5,V7=9

Immediately after data
read, before execution
of first recode statement

V6	V7	R1
5	9	1.5×10^9

After statement 1

V6	V7	R1
5	9	1

After statement 2

V6	V7	R1
5	2	1

After statement 3

V6	V7	R1
3	2	1

Fig. 6.5.   Example of Recoding Steps

6.8 Nine Sample Variable Transformation Problems Using the
Campus Unrest Data and OSIRIS Recode Statements

Unrest Data and OSIRIS Recode Statements

1. Compute the average speed at which a respondent travels to the
   nearest city. (V25 is the distance, V26 is the length of time
   it takes).

(i) For use in floating point mode

IF MDATA (V25,V26) OR V26 EQ 0 THEN R1=MD1(R1) ELSE R1=V25/V26

(ii) For use in integer mode

IF MDATA(V25,V26) OR V26 EQ 0 THEN R1=MD1(R1) -
ELSE R1=(V25*10)/V26

In both cases, missing data on either of the variables or a zero
divisor would cause an invalid computation. These conditions are
therefore first tested and the result set to missing data if any of
them are true. Otherwise the computation is performed.

If floating point mode is being used, the value of V26 reflects the
decimal place and no scaling is required. The results will have
the fractional part retained.

If integer mode is being used, the one implied decimal place indicated in the dictionary for V26 is ignored. The numerator is
therefore multiplied by 10 to adjust for this. The result will be
truncated to the nearest integer.

2. Collapse the education variable into three categories: no high
   school, high school, college.

   R2=BRAC(V8,0=0,1-6=1,7-9=2,>9=3)

This statement stores a value of 0,1, 2 or 3 in R2 according to the
value of V8. If V8 is 0 (missing data), R2 becomes 0; if V8 is in the
range 1-6 (no high school education), R2 becomes 1; if V8 is in the range
7-9 (high school education), R2 becomes 2; otherwise R2 is set to 3.

3. Collapse occupation into three categories--high status, medium
   status and low status occupations.

   R3=BRAC(V9,1-2=3,10=3,3-5=2,9=2,6-8=1,ELSE=0)

Professionals, managers and students are considered high status (result
value 3); sales, clerical, craftsmen, farmers are considered medium status
(result value 2); operatives, service workers, and labourers are considered
low status (result value 1); all other categories give a result value of 0
(missing data).

4. Form a status inconsistency index from education and occupation
   as follows:

   1 Low on education and occupation status, medium on both
       or high on both

70

2 Medium on one and either high or low on the other

3 Low on one and high on the other

0 Missing data on either or both variables

This index can be represented in a table where the rows and the columns of the table give the values of the two variables being combined (education and occupation) and the values in the cells of the table are the values to be assigned to the index:

Occupation	0	1	2	3
Education 0	0	0	0	0
1	0	1	2	3
2	0	2	1	2
3	0	3	2	1

R4=RECODE R2,R3,(1/1)(2/2)(3/3)=1,(2/1,3)(1,3/2)=2,(1/3)(3/1)=3,ELSE=0

The above statement using the RECODE function achieves the desired result. For each possible pair of values for R2 and R3, a unique result value is given. The values for the two variables are separated by slashes; alternative pairs of values which will take the same result are separated by parentheses, i. e. , the sample statement says: if (R2=1 and R3=1) or (R2=2 and R3=2) or (R2=3 and R3=3) then R4=1; if (R2=2 and R3=1 or 3) or (R2=1 or 3 and R3=2) then R4=2; if (R2=1 and R3=3) or (R2=3 and R3=1) then R4=3; if any other combination of values for R2 and R3 is encountered, then R4=0.

5. Variables 19-22 are four items from the Srole Anomie Scale. Anomie, according to Robinson and Shawn, is viewed as an individual's generalized pervasive state of social malintegration. An index of anomie is obtained by counting the number of unequivocal agreements on each of the four questions. Thus the index will range from 0 (no agreements) to 4 (all agreements).

    R5=COUNT(2,V19-V22)

This statement says 'count the number of 2's (the code for agree) occurring in the four variables V19, V20, V21, V22 for one case and place the result in R5.

6. Three dichotomous, or dummy, variables for marital status are to be constructed as follows

    (i) Not married/married   (V6 not equal 1/V6=1)
    (ii) Not single/single   (V6 not equal 2/V6=2)
    (iii) Not divorced or widowed/divorced, (V6 not equal 3/V6=3)
          widowed

        DUMMY R7-R9 USING V6 (1) (2) (3) ELSE 9

71

This statement says: if V6=1 (the first value specified), then R7=1 (the first result specified) and R8=0 and R9=0. If V6=2 (the second value specified), then R8=1 (the second result specified) and R7=0 and R9=0. If V6=3, then R9=1 and R7=0 and R8=0. If V6 takes any other value then R7, R8, and R9 will all be set to 9. The possible values (or sets of values) for V6 must be mutually exclusive so that only one of the dummy variables being created will ever get set to 1 for a given case.

7. Take the mean of variables 19-21, allowing up to 1 missing data value. If more than 1 of the variables are missing, then set the result to missing data. R10 is used to accumulate the count of cases with valid data, i.e., N. R11 is used to accumulate the sum.

```
MDATA R6(9.9)
R10=0
R11=0
IF NOT MDATA(V19) THEN R10=R10+1 AND R11=R11+V19
IF NOT MDATA(V20) THEN R10=R10+1 AND R11=R11+V20
IF NOT MDATA(V21) THEN R10=R10+1 AND R11=R11+V21
IF R10 LT 2 THEN R6=MD1(R6) ELSE R6=R11/R10
```

8. Set missing data codes for the R-type variable created in examples 1, 4, 6 and 7 above.

```
MDATA R4(0), R7(,9), R8(,9), R9(,9) R1(999.0), R6(9.9)
```

This example sets the first missing data code for result 4 to 0 and for result 1 to 999.0. For results 7, 8 and 9, a second missing data code of 9 is set. Decimals should not be specified if an integer analysis program is being used.

9. Set names for all R-type variables created in examples 1 and 4-7 above (names can be up to 24 characters long)

```
NAME R1 'TRAVEL SPEED TO CITY', R4 'STATUS INCONSISTENCY', -
R5 'ANOMIE', R7'MARRIED', R8 'SINGLE', R9 'DIVORCED' -
R6 'MEAN V19-V21'
```

The statements described in 1-9 above are all drawn together into one &RECODE setup in the example setup for the &TRANS file creation command described in second 6.12.

6.9 Testing OSIRIS Recode Syntax and Logic

There are two distinct kinds of errors that can be made with recoding statements. First, there are syntax errors--commas in the wrong places, spelling errors, statement structure errors. These errors are detected by the &RECODE command as the statements are read, and prior to the execution of the program with which they are being used. When working in batch mode, once an error is detected in a statement, no more checking of that statement is performed. However the rest of the statements are checked before the run is terminated. Syntax errors are reported on the printout as they are detected. When working from a terminal, if an error is detected, &RECODE will print a message and ask for a replacement statement. However, because &RECODE can not detect certain errors until the setup is complete

it is best to store the statements in a file when working at a terminal.
See Appendix [G].

Recode statements which are correct syntactically may well not be logi-
cally correct. That is, they look perfectly respectable to the recode
interpreter but they do not construct new variables in the way the user intended. Thus the statement: R1=V6/V7 looks perfectly alright. If,
however, the user meant to divide Variable 6 by Variable 8 (not Variable 7)
the values for R1 will not be what was intended.

Since writing a set of recode statements is like writing a computer
program, and since writing a computer program without logical errors at the
first try is an extremely rare occurrence, a short test on a set of recode
statements is recommended before embarking on a lengthy analysis run. One
way of doing this is by using the &DSLIST command, specifying a subset of
the data cases. The required set of recode statements can be input with
this command. The computer will then read and process a few cases, printing the values of the variables for each case after recoding. These values
can then be checked by the user. If they appear correct, the set of recode
statements can then be put with the setup for the required command and run.
An example of using &DSLIST in this way is given in Appendices B and C.

6.10 Common Errors Encountered With Recode, Their Reasons and Cures

a) Syntax Errors

The syntax for each recode statement has to be exactly correct.
Particularly common errors of this kind that are made are:

(i) Starting statements in column 1 instead of column 2

(ii) Using result values in a BRAC statement that are not simple
constants, i.e., one may not say:

ELSE=MD1(R1) in a bracket - e.g.,
R1=BRAC(V6,0-2=1,3=2,ELSE=MD1(R1))

(iii) Typing more than one statement on one line (or card)

Note: Some kinds of errors result in such confusion for the RECODE
scanner that it thinks there are errors in subsequent
statements when these are in fact good.

b) Errors and Warnings Concerned with Default Values

(i) All R-type variables (except R-type CARRY variables) are initialized to the constant 1.5×10^9 at the beginning of processing of
each case. If the set of recode statements bypass some recoding
steps under certain conditions, then R-type variables which do not
have a value assigned will have the value of 1.5×10^9 for that
case.

(ii) When a BRAC table is defined, the ELSE value is included as part
of the table. When a RECODE or TABLE is defined, the ELSE is not
included and instead must be specified as part of each assignment
statement that uses the table (or else the default value is assigned - see iii below).

(iii) TABLE and BRAC have a default value of 99 (i.e., ELSE defaults to 99).

RECODE has no default value. New values will only be assigned the result variable when a condition is satisfied. Otherwise of the result variable will be unchanged by the statement. This feature allows for partial recoding with RECODE, e.g., V2=RECODE V2, (1)=0 will set values of 1 of variable 2 equal to 0 but will leave all others unchanged. If the variable on the left side of the statement is an R-type variable (or a different V-type variable), then the initial value will be 1.5×10^{7} (or the value of that V-type variable for the case), which is what will remain after a RECODE state ment if a particular input values is not specified in the RECODE statement.

With BRAC partial recoding is not possible. V2=BRAC (V2,1=0) will set a value of 0 to variable 2 when its input value is 1 but in all other cases will cause the default ELSE value of 99 to be stored in variable 2.

(iv) Missing data values

Missing data values can be set in three different ways:

Specific MDATA statements can be used to set missing data values for R-type values and change missing data values for V-type variables.

If no MDATA statement exists for an R-type variable, a default value of 1.5×10^{7} is used as the first missing data code for data values and 1.6×10^{7} is used for the second missing data code. However, if a dictionary is being created (for example with command &TRANS), the first and second missing data will be left blank.

If no MDATA statement exists for a V-type variable, the missing data codes from the dictionary are used for that variable.

c) Fractional Results

There are two particular points over which the user should take care (see also section 6.6):

(i) Statements of the form

R1=V6/V7

will produce a different result when &RECODE is used in integer mode than when it is used in floating point mode. This is especially noticeable if V7 > V6 in which case the result will always be zero in integer mode but will take a fractional value in floating point mode.

When using &RECODE in integer mode in conjunction with
integer programs, it might be preferable to write

R1=V6x100/V7

thereby scaling the result up by 100 in
order to retain two decimal places.

(ii) Bracketing fractional values in floating point mode.

If a result produced by a recode statement is subsequently
bracketed, great care must be taken to ensure that all values
are accounted for:

R1=V6/V7
R2=BRAC(V6,0-1.0=1,1.1-2.0=2,2.1-10.0=3)

Since fractional numbers are not recorded exactly in the
computer, it is possible that all results to the first
statement actually lie between 1.0 and 1.1 or 2.0 and 2.1.
It is therefore much safer to write the bracket statement:

R2=BRAC(R1,<1.1=1,<2.1=2,ELSE=3)

(iii) Treatment of variables that have decimal places indicated in the
dictionary.

The actual values used for variables that have decimal places
indicated in the dictionary depend on whether an integer or
floating point mode is being used. If integer mode is used,
all data processing, including recoding is done treating the
values as integers and ignoring the decimal places.
Floating point mode on the other hand used values with the
correct number of decimals.

For example, suppose a three digit variable has two
implied decimal places and it is required to bracket it. The
bracket statement will be different according to whether the
statement is being used in integer or floating point mode:

R1=BRAC(V6,<100=1,<500=2,ELSE=3)

R1=BRAC(V6,<1.0=1,<5.0=2,ELSE=3)

d) Using V-type variables for storing results.

It is perfectly acceptable to store results in V-type
variables. This is often done, in particular, with the BRAC
function when result of bracketing a variable often replaces
the original value of that variable for a case, e.g.,

V2=BRAC(V2,0-10=1,11-15=2,ELSE=3)

Any variable that is in the input dictionary may be used on
the left side of the statement. However, it must be remembered
that its name and missing data codes will be as given in the
input dictionary unless changed by NAME and MDATA statements.
If the recoding is temporary, i.e., the results are being used

75

for analysis but not being retained, then the field width and
number of decimals in the input dictionary for the result
variable are ignored. If the &TRANS command is being
used to output new variables, then the field width and number
decimals are used in the construction of the output dictionary.

In general, it is recommended that results be stored
on R-type variables in order to avoid potential problems
of using random V-type variables.

6.11 Creation of Permanent Data Files Containing Recoded Variables

When recoding statements such as described in sections 6.3-6.7 are written and used, no permanent record of the created variables is kept. New
variables are merely constructed as each input data record is read, used to
augment management or analysis results internally, and then overwritten in
the memory by the new variables for the next input data record. There is
however a method in OSIRIS for creating and keeping new variables. The
&TRANS (transformation) command is used in conjunction with OSIRIS recode
statements to output data records instead of augmenting management or
analysis results. &TRANS operates case by case creating new variables
based on the values of old variables in one data case. It automatically
creates an output dictionary to describe the new data file.

OSIRIS also contains an aggregation program, called &AGGREG, which can
be used to construct new variables based on values of variables taken
across a set of cases. It is discussed in section 6.13.[10]

6.12 The OSIRIS &TRANS (Transformation) Command

The setup for the &RECODE-&TRANS run consists of the &RECODE command,
recode statements, the &TRANS command (including input and output assignments), and &TRANS control statements. An example is given below of an
&TRANS setup to output data records consisting of all the original variables of the Campus Unrest data along with the seven variables created by
the recode statements described in section 6.8. &TRANS can output new
variables in regular character mode or alternatively in a number of other
modes of which integer or floating point binary mode (binary means a special representation of numbers convenient to computers but not comprehen-
sible to people) are potentially the most useful. Binary output mode is
sometimes used in order to make processing of the file cheapter later. The
default output mode is the mode of the input variable. The default input
made for R-type variables is floating binary with two decimals. If character output is desired, it must be explicitly specified. Character mode
must be used if the data are to be accessed outside of OSIRIS, e.g., in
MIDAS or SPSS.

On the &TRANS parameter card, four parameters are given. 'R=1' says to
apply the set of recode statements just preceding; since those recode
statements weren't given a special number with a recode statement, they are
by default number '1'. 'P=OUTD' says to print the output dictionary.
'TYPE=C' specifies that all output variables should be character mode. The

---

[10]For very special variable transformation, it is sometimes more efficient
to write a special purpose program in a language such as FORTRAN [5] or
UC360 [4].

```
$CREATE CUDI7
$CREATE CUDA7
$RUN ISR:OSIRIS.IV
&RECODE
 IF MDATA(V25,V26) OR V26 EQ 0 THEN R1=MD1(R1) ELSE R1=V25/V26
 R2=BRAC(V8,0=0,1-6=1,7-9=2,>9=3)
 R3=BRAC(V9,1-2=3,10=3,3-5=2,9=2,6-8=1,ELSE=0)
 R4=RECODE R2,R3,(1/1)(2/2)(3/3)=1,(2/1,3)(1,3/2)=2, -
   (1/3)(3/1)=3,ELSE=0
 R5=COUNT(2,V19-V22)
 DUMMY R7-R9 USING V6(1) (2) (3) ELSE 9
 R10=0
 R11=0
 IF NOT MDATA(V19) THEN R10=R10+1 AND R11=R11+V19
 IF NOT MDATA(V20) THEN R10=R10+1 AND R11=R11+V20
 IF NOT MDATA(V21) THEN R10=R10+1 AND R11=R11+V21
 IF R10 LT 2 THEN R6=MD1(R6) ELSE R6=R11/R10
 MDATA R4(0), R7(,9) R8(,9) R9(,9) R1(999.9), R6(9.9)
 NAME R1 'TRAVEL SPEED TO CITY', R4 'STATUS INCONSISTENCY', -
 R5 'ANOMIE', -
 R7 'MARRIED', R8 'SINGLE', R9'DIVORCED', R6'MEAN V19-V21'
&END
&TRANS DICTIN=DI4 DATAIN=DA4 DICTOUT=CUDI7 DATAOUT=CUDA7
CREATING A NEW FILE CONTAINING VARIABLES FROM SECTION 6.8     Label
R=1 P=OUTD TYPE=C V=1-33,R1,R4-R9 RENU=1                      Parameter Stmt.
V=R4,R5,R7-R9 WI=1 NDEC=0                                     Dictionary
V=R1 WI=4 NDEC=1                                              Specifica-
V=R6 WI=2 NDEC=1                                              tion Stmts.
&END
```

'V=' keyword is used to list the variables which are to be output. The
renumbering keyword must be specified--the R variables will simply become
variables 34-40. Dictionary Specification Statements are optional; they
are used to override defaults for either old or new variables. In this
case we want the original variables just as they were, which is the
default. However we elect to override the default for the R variables; by
default the R variables would be floating point binary with a width of 4
with 2 decimal places.

After this job has been run, the original dictionary and data files will
remain and a new data file will exist, along with a dictionary to describe
it, containing, for each case, the original variables 1-33 along with 7 new
variables (R1,R4-R9).

As new variables are generated, each additional variable should be added
to the working codebook. New variables should be accompanied by the conditions of their generation as well as their code values. For example, if an
'anomie' index was constructed and added to the Campus Unrest data, the
methods and conditions of its generation should be recorded.

6.13 Computing Aggregate Items with OSIRIS

    Section 6.12 discussed the creation and storage of new variables for in-
dividual data cases based on the values of existing variables. Computing
new variables based on values of variables across sets of cases is known as
aggregation or summarization. For instance, in the Campus Unrest data one
could compute mean values of certain variables across all cases in a par-

ticular state; one would then be aggregating by state. The command in
OSIRIS for doing this is &AGGREG. (See footnote to section 6.11.) Simple
aggregation can also be accomplished in OSIRIS by use of &RECODE.

&AGGREG

&AGGREG aggregates an input file, grouping records according to the
value of a specified ID field, computes aggregate values of variables and
outputs a new file (or, in some cases, multiple files) containing one data
record for each group of input records (e.g., for each state in the Campus
Unrest Data). The input data must be in order by ID or must be sorted by
$AGRREG (using the SORT Keyword on the parameter statement). Analysis can
then be performed at a new level, the state level, as opposed to the individual level or the aggregated values can be merged back onto the
original records. For example:

```
$CREATE DI8
$CREATE DA8
$RUN ISR:OSIRIS.IV
&AGGREG DICTIN=DI4 DATAIN=DA4 DICTOUT=DI8 DATAOUT=DA8
AGGREGATING CAMPUS UNREST DATA                          Label
PRINT=OUTD                                              Parameter Stmt.
ID=1 VSTART=1 VARS=7,8,23,25 STAT=(MIN,MAX,SUM,MEAN,N)  File parameter
&END                                                   statement
```

The Parameter Statement simply requests the printing of the output dictionary. The File Parameter Statement describes one output file. There
may be more than one File Parameter Statement in a setup. Here we are
creating one file. Variable 1 is the State code. By naming this the ID
variable, on the file parameter statement, all records with the same state
code will be taken as one group. For each of the variables in the V=list,
the sum, mean, minimum, maximum and count of non-missing data values will
be computed over all the records with the same state ID. A record will be
output to the new file containing these 20 values (5 statistics for each of
4 variables) along with the value of the state ID; the next group of
records will then be processed. The output data file will contain only 5
records, one for each state in the data, each record containing 21 variables.

Once one has an aggregated datast one can do analysis at that new level
or one can use &UPDATE to combine the new aggregate data with the original
dataset; in this later case the output dataset would contain one record for
each of the individual input records, with the aggregated items added to
each relevant record along with variable values transferred from the input
records. This combination file can then be used in conjunction with OSIRIS
recoding where, for instance, Z-scores are required or where the distance
of an individual's value for a particular variable from some index for a
group to which he belongs is of analytical interest. A pictorial representation of the various files is given in Figure 6.6.

Suppose it were desired to perform an analysis with a variable which
gave the difference between a person's age and the mean age for the state
in which the person lives; one could use a file created by &UPDATE that
combined output from &AGGREG and the original file as the input data along
with a RECODE statement of the form

        IF V4 EQ 1 THEN R1=V36-V7 ELSE R1=V37-V7

This statement would set R1 to be the difference between the mean age of men or women for the state and the respondent's age depending on the sex of the respondent.

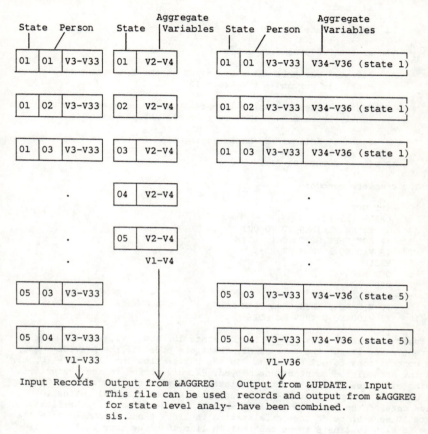

Fig. 6.6 Input and Output Files for Aggregation

6.14 Aggregation with &RECODE

The trick to using &RECODE for aggregation is the CARRY statement. The pitfalls are processing the first and last case. The following example sums the unemployed (code 2 on V10) for each state. In the following recode

R1   contains code of last state read (the CARRY statement intializes R1 to 0; since R1 was intialized by CARRY it is not reintialized each time a case is read)

79

R2   contains count of unemployed so far for this current state
(the CARRY statement intializes R2 to 0; since R2 was
intialized by CARRY it is <u>not</u> reintialized each time a case
is read)

V1   is the State Variable

V10 is the Employment Variable

R100 "output" variable which is passed to the management or
analysis command - the State ID

R200 "output" variable which is passed to the management or
analysis command - the count of the unemployed

In the code that follows the basic aggregation is the 4th line

IF V10 EQ 2 THEN R2=R2+1

The complete recode:

```
       &RECODE
    1  CARRY (R1,R2)
    2  IF R1 NE V1 THEN GO TO OUT
    3  IF EOF THEN GO TO OUT
    4  IF V10 EQ 2 THEN R2=R2+1
    5  REJECT
    6  OUT R100=R1
    7  R200=R2
    8  R1=V1
    9  IF V10 EQ 2 THEN R2=1 ELSE R2=0
   10  IF R100 EQ 0 THEN REJECT
```

Every time there is a <u>change</u> in the state ID, i.e., V1, state ID for
current case, is not the same as R1, the state code for the previous case,
the control goes to OUT (line 2). In the OUT section the old state ID, R1,
and the accumulated count of unemployed, R2, are copied to the "output"
variables (lines 6 and 7). R1 is reintialized with the new state ID and
the count of unemployed in R2 is begun again (lines 8 and 9). Line 10
takes care of the start up problem: when R1 changes from 0 to the first
state ID we want to do the intialization in lines 8 and 9 (and we need the
copy to R100 in line 6 so we can test in line 10 - the copy in line 7 is
harmless), but we do <u>not</u> want to pass values (R100=0,R200=0) to the management or analysis command. If R100 is 0 i.e., old state ID is 0, we REJECT
(line 10). The REJECT command goes and gets a new case without passing
values to the command. Note we also REJECT at line 5, after a normal ac-
cumulation. The last case problem is tackled in line 3: when the end of
file is detected control is transferred to OUT, the output variables are
set, the reintialization is harmless, and, since R100 won't be equal to 0,
R100 and R200 are passed to the management or analysis command. Most users
prefer &AGGREG.

6.15 Summary

The variables collected by a researcher are very often not in the exact
form that is suitable for analysis. Modification or transformations of the
original variables have to be performed. This can be done either on a temporary or a permanent basis. Temporary in this context means that vari-

80

ables are created for a particular command for the duration of that run only. Permanent means that the new values are recorded on a data file for future use. The most common kind of variable construction is performed on values within each data case. These new values are based on existing data for that case. Sometimes, however, new values are computed based on data values across a set of cases. With OSIRIS, within case variable transformation is perfomed by the OSIRIS recoding facility. In conjunction with most OSIRIS commands the variable transformation is temporary. It can, however, be used with the transformation command (&TRANS) to create a permanent file containing old and new variables. Across case variable transformations can be performed in two ways - by the &AGGREG command or by &RECODE together with &TRANS or some other command. &AGGREG produces a file of summary or aggregated values. These then have to be merged back into individual data cases if relationships between individual and aggregated values are required. Aggregation with &RECODE is a bit tricky, but possible.

Chapter 7

DATA ANALYSIS

7.1 Nature of Data

The basic data for virtually all statistical analysis programs consist of the values of a set of variables observed for each respondent in a sample. The term "respondent," as used here, may refer to a household, a business firm, a county, etc.; it is the basic unit of study, and is better called a case. We think of each variable as being measured for each case; if a measurement is missing or inapplicable for a particular case that is indicated by a designated numeric code (a missing data code).

The choice of an appropriate technique depends on the goals of the analysis, the relationships among the variables, and the scale of measurement of the variables. Scale of measurement refers to the assumptions one makes about the properties of a variable—in particular, whether a variable is nominal, ordinal or interval. See section 2.11.

Frequently, statistical summaries of a sample may be more meaningfully calculated with a weight (a significance multiplier) assigned to each case. Weights may be desirable for a variety of reasons, including varying response rates and sampling fractions. (See section 2.6.) These weights are represented by a variable generated for the purpose and are routinely utilized by OSIRIS in computing sample statistics.

Another characteristic of each OSIRIS statistical analysis program is its treatment of missing data. Typically, each statistic is calculated from all of the available observations, so that the number of observations may vary among statistics because of missing data. Details regarding each program's treatment of missing data are available in the program writeups in the OSIRIS IV Manual.

All of the OSIRIS statistical commands can be used, if desired, to analyze a subset of the original sample. A subset is characterized as those cases for which one or more variables satisfy prescribed conditions. In OSIRIS this process of case selection is called filtering.

7.2 Data Analysis with OSIRIS

The OSIRIS package contains programs for a wide range of statistical analysis techniques. These include univariate analysis (frequency distributions or marginals and summary statistics such as the mean, mode, median) performed on single variables; bivariate analysis such as two way frequency distributions, one way analysis of variance, simple linear regression and correlation; multivariate analysis involving more than two variables such as multiple regression and multivariate analysis of variance techniques, clustering, and scaling techniques. A description of each of the OSIRIS analysis commands can be found in Appendix [I].

In this Chapter, we will discuss only two OSIRIS analysis commands. The most commonly used analysis command in the package is the &TABLES command. This command can be used to compute univariate distributions and summary statistics, bivariate distributions and associated summary statistics, and can also be used to produce three and four way tables.

The second command discussed is the OSIRIS missing data correlation command, &MDC. Some OSIRIS programs require as input not the normal OSIRIS dataset of raw data scores but instead a matrix of coefficients relating variables, such as correlation coefficients which are produced by &MDC. The clustering and scaling programs in OSIRIS, for example, require a correlation matrix as input. Matrices in OSIRIS are in a special format.

Use of any analysis command requires a knowledge of the particular analytical technique for which the program is designed in order to select the appropriate options. However, once the options have been chosen, setting up the computer run is a relatively simple process.

7.3 The OSIRIS &TABLES Command

&TABLES produces weighted or unweighted univariate or bivariate cross tabulations. A univariate distribution is simply the distribution of all cases across the values of a given variable. For example when requesting the univariate distribution of V4 'Sex' the program might print out the fact that in the total N of 23, 9 are coded 1 (male) and 14 are coded 2 (female). Besides frequencies one can also obtain percentages and univariate descriptive statistics, for example, mean, median, mode, skewness, kurtosis, etc. Synonyms for univariate distributions are marginals and frequencies.

Many researchers run &TABLES directly after creating an OSIRIS dataset to produce univariate distributions on most variables. This is an elementary but very good check of one's data. With these tables, one can check whether the data are consistent with original expectations. For example, if one looks at variable 4 'Sex' and finds that the code categories range from 0-9, one can be sure that a mistake occured at some point in the file creation process. Likewise, univariate distributions are used by many projects as a pre-WILD CODE CHECK. That is, one can tell by looking at the variables accessed whether or not there are code values that are not legitimate, i.e., "wild". Time and money can be saved by wild code checking (with &WCC) only those variables known to have "wild codes". It is unnecessary to waste time checking variables that are already known to be correct.

For the same reasons, the running of univariate distributions after the creation of new variables e.g., after &RECODE and &TRANS, is highly recommended.

Bivariate distributions or cross tabulations are the tabulation of two or more variables together. That is, a bivariate table represents the count of the number of cases in which specific values on the tabulated variables are shared. One variable is usually referred to as the row, or strata, variable and the second as the column, or spread, variable. A hypothetical cross tabulation of var 4 'Sex' and Var 5 'race' follows:

Figure 7.1 illustrates how a total sample of 300 is distributed across the two variables, race and sex. Each cell of the table represents the sharing of two codes by a number of units, e.g., 117 cases have a '1' on V4 and '1' on V5.

Cross tabulations depict the relationships between two variables. In the social sciences the search is often for a predictive model; certain variables are called predictor or independent variables and other dependent variables. Bivariate tables are often employed to test the relationship

84

		Var 5 'Race'			
Var 4 'Sex'		1 White	2 Black	3 Other	
Male	1	117	20	10	147
Female	2	119	25	9	153
		236	45	19	300

Fig. 7.1 Hypothetical Cross Tabulation of Sex and Race

between two variables. Usually these relationships are outlined and anticipated in advance. For example, the hypothesis that sex affects the occupation a person selects can be tested with a bivariate table. If there is no relationship between the two variables one would expect each cell in the table to reflect the distribution of each variable in the general population. Two tables follow: both are bivariate tables—cross tabulting sex and occupation (our hypothetical sample contains only four occupations).

Figure 7.2a indicates that there is no relationship between sex and occupation in our sample; each occupation reflects the general 50-50 split of males and females in the sample.

Column Variable 2 Occupation

Row Variable 1 Sex		Doctor	Nurse	Secretary	Carpenter	
a)	Male	10	10	15	15	50
	Female	10	10	15	15	50
		20	20	30	30	100

		Doctor	Nurse	Secretary	Carpenter	
b)	Male	16	5	0	29	50
	Female	4	15	30	1	50
		20	20	30	30	100

Fig. 7.2. Two Hypothetical Relationships Between Sex and Occupational Choice

Figure 7.2b suggests that being male or female does affect one's occupational choice. There are many statistics available in &TABLES which measure the strength of a relationship in a sample and the probability that the variables are related in the larger population. The researcher selects statistics depending on the nature of the data and the properties of various statistics.

In Figures 7.2a and 7.2b it is easy to distinguish the independent and dependent variables; temporally, sex is obviously the predictor variable and occupation, the dependent variable (sex is established much before one's occupation). It is not always necessary to distinguish between the independent and dependent variables. However, when it is possible to iden- tify one variable as the predictor, percentages are usually requested within categories of the predictor variable; for example, if the predictor was a row variable, row percentages would be requested. With reference to Figure 7.2b one would say that 30% of the females in our sample chose nurs- ing as a profession. (Note that there are three ways of computing per- centages: using row totals, column totals and grand totals respectively.)

A sample of &TABLES is given below:

```
$RUN ISR:OSIRIS.IV
&RECODE
  R1=BRAC(V25, 0-5=1, 6-10=2, 11-20=3, 21-50=4, 51-100=5, -
  101-500=6, 501-998=7,999=9)
  IF V4 EQ 1 AND V9 INLIST (1-4) THEN R2=1          Recode Stmts.
  NAME R1' DIST FRM CITY COLAPSD', R2 'MALE WC'
  MDATA R1 (,9)
&END
&TABLES DICTIN=DI4 DATAIN=DA4
AN EXAMPLE OF A TABLES RUN ON CAMPUS UNREST DATA   Label
R=1 PRINT=DICT                                     Parameter Stmt.
V=11 DEL=MD1 P=ROW% REPE=(V8=1-5/6-11/6-9)         Analysis Stmts.
V=28 S=4 DEL=MD1 REPE=(V8=1-11) P=ROW% STAT=ORD
V=15-20
V=22 S=6,9 DEL=MD1 P=ROW% STAT=CHI REPE=(V7=16-25/26-50/51-98)
V=14 S=R1 REPE=(R2=1) DEL=(MD1,MD2) STAT=ORD
&END
```

&TABLES, like many OSIRIS commands, starts with an optional global fil- ter (not used in the above example), followed by a mandatory label and a mandatory parameter statement. In &TABLES, one can on the parameter state- ment, among other things, specify what the program is to do when bad data (e.g., blanks in a numeric variable) are encountered, set the suffix for the input data file, select printing options, invoke a set of recode state- ments, and specify a weight variable. In the example, we have invoked a set of recode statements numbered 1, and asked to have the dictionary printed. If bad data are encountered, the default will take effect (MD1 for that variable will be substituted--or, if the variable doesn't have a MD1 code in the dictionary, the number 1.5 billion). The default suffix, IN, was used in the input file assignment. There is no weight variable in this run.

7.4 &TABLES Analysis Statements

The five analysis statements are the meat of the setup. The tabulations desired are specified using these statements. Options are selected by specifying keywords followed by a list of the selected options. A list of some of the more important keywords is given in Figure 7.3. The simplest way to describe a table is by defining it in one analysis statement (it is permissible for an analysis statement to extend over more than one line; use a dash for continuation). The row (strata) and column variables are specified along with the options for a given table. If no strata variable

86

is specified, the table is assumed to be univariate. The first two table descriptor lines in our example:

V=11 DEL=MD1 P=ROW% REPE=(V8=1-5/6-11/6-9)
V=28 S=4 DEL=MD1 REPE=(V8=1-11) P=ROW% STAT=ORD

describe two tables. The first line describes a univariate distribution for a single variable with row percentages repeated on each of the three subsets defined by the repetition factor. The second line describes a single bivariate table with row percentages for the single subset defined by the repetition factor. A repetition factor is a fast way to generate multiple tables or three way tables: it is in essence a multiple filter. Subsets of cases are separated by slashes in the REPE keyword. The first statement requests three univariate distributions of v11--one for cases that have less than 9 grades of education, one for cases that have 9 or more grades of education, and one for cases that have 9-12 grades of education. Note that the subsets need not be exclusive. The second statement requests a bivariate, or two-way, table; in addition to the V= keyword there is a S= keyword. In a bivariate table, V= is used for column variables and S= is used for row variables. This statement shows use of the REPE= keyword as a filter: here a single subset is defined--cases with non-missing values for Education. In both statements, DEL=MD1 has been specified, which requests that missing data be omitted from all percentage and statistical calculations. Regardless of any DEL= setting, data are always (unless filtered out) <u>printed</u> in the table so that the researcher can see them. DEL= has only to do with missing data in calculations. Ordinal statistics have been requested for the bivariate table; this request will result in Kendall's tau a, tau b, tau c, and Goodman and Kruskal's gamma being printed beneath the frequency table.

Tables may also be mass generated. This method is used, for example, when one wants to generate a number of tables all with the same options. Mass generation of tables usually reduces the amount of typing time at a terminal. Mass generation of univariate tables is accomplished by giving a list of variable numbers on the V= keyword. Mass generation of bivariate tables is accomplished by giving a list for either the S=keyword or the V=keyword or both. The following statement would result in 200 (10 x 4 x 5) bivariate tables:

The third analysis statement in the example above requests six univariate distributions. The fourth statement requests three bivariate tables, each for three subsets. The last table requested--

V=14 S=R1 REPE=(R2=1) DEL=(MD1,MD2) STAT=ORD

requests a single bivariate table with an R type variable, previously defined in the &RECODE instructions, as the row variable. Since, in the recode, we set '9' equal to the second MDATA code (note the ',' before the '9' in the MDATA statement) we set DEL=(MD1,MD2) to delete missing data on either V14 or R1. When more than one value follows a keyword such as DEL= they must be enclosed in parentheses. This statement also uses a result variable defined in the recode as a filter in the REPE=. The REPE= keyword can only reference a single variable or result variable. Here we wanted a filter for white collar males, a combination of two variables, sex and occupation. The filter variable, R2, was constructed in the recode statements and then used in the Analysis Statement.

V=11-20 S=3-6 REPE=(V100=1/2/3/4/5)

Option	&TABLE Keyword
univariate	V=(list)
column variable in bivariate	V=(list)
row variable in bivariate	S=(list)
eliminate MDATA?	DEL=(MD1,MD2)
repetition factor	REPE=(expressions)
percentages	PRINT=(ROW%,COL%,TOT%)
statistics	STATS=(list)

Fig. 7.3. Some Options and Keywords in the &TABLES Command.
(These keywords are all used in Analysis Statements.)

A keyword not used in our setup--and indeed seldom used--is the COMBINE keyword. It is appropriate when the researcher wants to treat a set of variables as a multiple response variable. In our data the seven newspaper variables can be treated as a multiple variable (to the question, "What daily newspapers do you read?"). (Each can also, of course, be treated as a single variable in its own right.) The &TABLES Analysis Statement

V=27-33 S=4 COM

would give a bivariate table showing Sex by Frequency of Reading Newspapers, all newspapers combined.

Variables 27-33 Frequency of Newspaper Reading

		1	2	3	9	Totals
Variable 4	1	26	47	113	10	196
Sex	2	15	30	99	10	154
Totals		41	77	212	20	350

Note that each of 50 cases in the data has been recorded in the table 7 times, making a total of 350 responses.

7.5 The OSIRIS Missing Data Correlations Command

The OSIRIS &MDC (missing data correlations) command is the second analysis command covered in this manual. It was selected for discussion because of its simple setup, which consists of an optional filter, a label, and a parameter statement, and also because it can produce a correlation matrix useable in other analysis runs. OSIRIS Matrices will be explained in section 7.6.

88

&MDC produces a matrix of Pearson product moment correlations. It can be an efficient way to input data to the &REGRESSN command and other OSIRIS commands that use variance - covariance or correlation matrices. The name of the program derives from the fact that it checks for missing data values, as defined in the input dictionary. Missing data is checked in either of two ways; pairwise or casewise. In pairwise checking, when a missing data code is detected in either of the two variables being correlated, that case is excluded only from that correlation. Note that the pairwise option checks for missing data codes within each pair of variables correlated. The casewise option, as in other analysis commands, for example, &REGRESSN, checks for missing data values at the case level; that is, if a case contains missing data values on any of the analysis variables it is totally excluded from the analysis run. Pairwise checking for missing data means that more cases are available to enter the analysis but is more time consuming because of the extra checking involved.

Pearson product moment correlations assume that the variables involved are interval or continuous and that the relationship between variables is linear. On the most general level, a correlation measures the degree to which two variables vary together. A value of 1.0 indicates a perfect correlation between two variables; for every change in one variable there is a corresponding change in its correlate. The perfect negative correlation is -1.0; for every increase on one variable there is a corresponding decrease in the other. Correlations fall within the range 1.0 to -1.0.

A setup with two &MDC commands follows:

```
$CREATE MYMAT
$RUN ISR:OSIRIS.IV
&MDC DICTIN=DI4 DATAIN=DA4 SPUNCH=MYMAT
EXCLUDE V24=0,9 AND V4=2 AND V7=<50 AND V7=>98          Filter
CORRELATIONS ON CU ATTUTUDES - MALES 50-98 - NO RURAL  Label
M=1 WRITE COR=SY DEL=PAIRS V=15-19                     Parameter Stmt.
&MDC SPUNCH=MYMAT(LAST+1)
EXCLUDE V24=0,9 AND V4=1 AND V7=>40                     Filter
CORRELATIONS ON CU ATTITUDES - FEMALES 0-40-NO RURAL   Label
M=2 WRITE V=15-19                                      Parameter Stmt.
&END
```

On the second &MDC command DICTIN= and DATAIN= were not respecified. We have taken advantage of the OSIRIS default that input dataset assignments stay in effect until changed.

In these setups filters have been used to define the subset of cases of interest. The filters are each followed by label cards. The parameters designate the selected options. The only parameter that is always necessary is V=, to select the variables to be correlated. In these setups we have elected to output the matrix to a permanent file. To make a permanent machine readable copy of the matrix, three things need to be done:

a) On the &MDC command, SPUNCH must be assigned to a file (if SPUNCH is assigned to *PUNCH* the matrix is punched on cards).
b) The keyword WRITE must be specified on the parameter card.
c) The output matrix must be numbered using the M= keyword unless the number 1, the default, is satisfactory.

On the first &MDC command we direct the program to output the matrix to the disk file MYMAT. On the second &MDC we direct the second matrix to the same file but tell the &MDC command to begin writing the second matrix at the last line plus one (LAST+1). After these two commands are executed the file MYMAT will contain two matrices. Note that WRITE appears on both parameter cards and that the matrices are numbered 1 and 2 (M=1 is not necessary on the parameter card for the first run). In a &REGRESSN setup, for example, either the first or second matrix can be retrieved by making the MYMAT file available (see section 7.6) and specifying M=1 or M=2 on the &REGRESSN parameter card.

If it is desired to have a machine readable output matrix only for use by a subsequent command in the same OSIRIS.IV run, then simply using the keyword M= will cause the matrix to be stored temporarily so that it can be used, say, by a &REGRESSN command or a &CLUSTER command.

If WRITE, SPUNCH and M= are not used, the matrix is printed on paper, but not saved in a form that a command can use.

On the first of the Parameter Statements, COR=SY and DEL=PAIRS were specified. These are the defaults for those keywords and the specification was not necessary. The COR= keyword is used to specify what combinations of variables are to be correlated. The default, symmetric, requests correlations between all pairs of variables in the list. The DEL= keyword allows the user to choose between pairwise or casewise elimination of missing data, as described above. There are keywords which control printing (PRINT=) and the precision (SINGLE or DOUBLE) used in calculations. The default is double precision which is conservative, though a bit more expensive than single precision. &MDC also has options to print or write the covariance matrix rather than the correlation matrix.

Each &MDC command in the sample setup will produce a printed 5 x 5 correlation matrix as well as a machine readable matrix in MYMAT. An example of a printed matrix is shown in Figure 7.4.

Var.	15	16	17	18
Var.				
16	0.0809			
17	0.0840	0.3790		
18	0.0667	0.1657	0.1712	
19	0.3109	-0.1511	-0.0379	-0.0330

Fig. 7.4. Printout of a 5 by 5 Correlation Matrix

Means and standard deviations are standard part of each matrix (printed or machine readable) produced by &MDC. The printing of measurements such as regression coefficients and cross product matrices is controlled by the PRINT= keyword.

7.6 OSIRIS Correlation Matrices

When a correlation matrix is output to a file or punched onto cards by &MDC it is very useful to have names and numbers included in the file. The

&MDC command automatically outputs the appropriate names and numbers. The
lines (or cards) containing the names and numbers precede the cards containing correlations, means, and standard deviations.

The file (i.e., MYMAT) produced by our sample setup is shown in Fig.
7.5.

To use an OSIRIS IV matrix in a subsequent run one must make it available to the analysis commands by using &MATRIX. If, for example, one
wanted to make the matrices stored in the file MYMAT available to &REGRESSN
in a run, one would place the command

&MATRIX SOURCE=MYMAT

in the setup before the &REGRESSN command. If one wanted to make matrices
stored on cards available to &REGRESSN one would include a &MATRIX card in
the setup immediately followed by the set of punched cards constituting the
OSIRIS matrix (i.e., the parameter statement, names, correlations, means
and standard deviations).

7.7 Other OSIRIS Matrices

Square matrices need not always contain Pearson product moment correlation coefficients; matrices of other types of coefficients can be used by
certain OSIRIS programs. For example, distance matrices or other types of
coefficients can be used by certain OSIRIS programs. For example, distance
matrices may be input into the &CLUSTER and &MINISSA commands. There is
currently no OSIRIS command which generates distance matrices but if one is
generated outside of OSIRIS (in MIDAS for example) it is not difficult to
arrange it in standard OSIRIS format.

Matrices can also be rectangular. The rectangular matrix differs from a
square matrix in that the number of row and column variables differ. This
distinction, i.e., row and column, is noted on the parameter statement.
Since the use of rectangular matrices is infrequent they will not be explained here. For further information on rectangular matrices see the
OSIRIS IV Manual [10].

```
a  [MAT=001 DIM=(005,000) NAME MF=(WIDTH=15 NDEC=8 TYPE=C) SF=(WIDTH=15 NDEC=8)
b  │    V15'STUDENT VOICE        014'      V16'CONSPIRACY           Q15'    M   1
   │    V17'BAN SDS              016'      V18'VIET NAM             Q17'    M   2
   └    V19'LOT OF AVERAGE MAN   018'                                      M   3
   ┌    .80865681E-01  .84005594E-01  .66710055E-01  .31091881E+00         M   4
   │    .37897032E+00  .16569871E+00 -.15106606E+00                        M   5
c  │    .17116976E+00 -.37859596E-01                                       M   6
   └   -.33035520E-01                                                      M   7
   ┌    .15106382E+01  .19782600E+01  .14468079E+01  .14375000E+01 .15957441E+01M  8
d  └    .58504325E+00  .53703421E+00  .50253743E+00  .61562109E+00 .49605280E+00M  9
     MAT=002 DIM=(005,000) NAME MF=(WIDTH=15 NDEC=8 TYPE=C) SF=(WIDTH=15 NDEC=8)
        V15'STUDENT VOICE        014'      V16'CONSPIRACY           Q15'    M   1
        V17'BAN SDS              016'      V18'VIET NAM             Q17'    M   2
        V19'LOT OF AVERAGE MAN   018'                                      M   3
        .83636343E-01  .48620742E-01  .40214609E-01  .27272725E+00         M   4
        .38391334E+00  .16746593E+00 -.15527862E+00                        M   5
        .14483893E+00 -.98058045E-01                                       M   6
       -.80124557E-01                                                      M   7
        .15333328E+01  .19777775E+01  .14666662E+01  .14565210E+01 .16222219E+01M  8
        .58775377E+00  .54309249E+00  .50452489E+00  .62205821E+00 .49031007E+00M  9
```

Fig. 7.5. A Machine Readable Output File Containing Two Matrices
Produced by &MDC command. This figure shows the contents of a disk
file; if the matrix had been punched on cards, each line would be
punched on a separate card. See the OSIRIS IV Manual [10].

a. This line, generated by &MDC, is the parameter statement for a subsequent &MATRIX command. MAT=001 indicates that '1' is the reference
number for this matrix. The DIM= keyword gives the row and column
dimensions; the column being '000' implies the matrix is symmetric.
NAMEs will be supplied. MF= gives the format of the correlations:
each correlation occupies a 15 column field, has 8 decimal places, and
is in character numeric mode. SF= gives the format for the means and
standard deviations.

b. These are variable numbers and names. &MDC extracts this information
from the input dictionary and creates these lines, two names to a
line, which are in the format appropriate for &MATRIX.

c. The correlation values appear on the next four lines (in columns
1-72). When the matrix is square, e.g., as produced by the &MDC command, the off diagonal, lower-left half of the matrix is punched
column-wise. That is, each column of the matrix is punched across a
line according to the first format record. For example, compare the
correlation matrix in Figure 7.4 with the same correlations formatted
in an output file in Figure 7.5; note that the first column of correlations in Figure 7.4 is punched across the first correlation line
in Figure 7.5. If one has more correlations in one column than will
fit on one line, the correlations are continued onto the next line.
The command that reads the file will adjust its reading to the correct
number of variables. Each new column of the matrix should start on a
new line.

The correlations are in E notation. This means that the fraction,
e.g., .80865681, should be multiplied by 10 to the power of the ex-
ponent (the number following the E). Thus .80865681E-01=.080856581.

d. The means appear on the first line and standard deviations on the
second. These statistics are retained as part of the square correlation matrix because they are required by many of the techniques that
utilize correlations, e.g., factor analysis.

The second matrix in this file follows the same pattern as the first.

92

Chapter 8

STRUCTURED FILES IN OSIRIS

8.1 Introduction

One of the most exciting - and interesting - features of OSIRIS IV is
its ability to handle hierarchical structured files. This chapter will
provide just the merest flavor of what they are and how they can be used.
Researchers seriously interested in structured files should consult (in addition to the OSIRIS IV Manual) OHDS: An Introduction to OSIRIS Hierarchical Data Structures [1]. Intended as a supplement to the OSIRIS IV Manual,
the OHDS Manual concentrates on the hierarchical data structures facility
in OSIRIS. Much of the material below has been copied or adapted from the
OHDS manual. Note however that the OHDS Manual is much more complete.
(The OHDS Manual was written in 1979. It is the first 52 pages that are
particularly recommended. The detailed, technical command writeups towards
the back of the manual are out-of-date).

8.2 Overview of Creating and Using Structured Datasets

Thus far in this text, we have meant by OSIRIS dataset a standard OSIRIS
dataset. As the reader well knows by now, a standard OSIRIS dataset consists of two files, one for the dictionary and another for the data. The
dictionary file contains descriptive information about each of the variables in the data file. The records in the data file are all of the same
fixed length and contain the same variables in the same locations. This is
commonly called a flat, or rectangular, file; it has no variation in its
record structure. Suppose, however, that we have three separate standard
OSIRIS datasets, one with data on individual adult respondents, a second
with data on their children, and a third with data on the children's medical incidents. And suppose we want all of this data together in such a way
as to allow us to do analysis on any of the variables or a combination of
variables. To this end, we can combine these datasets into a single structured dataset. The data from each of the standard OSIRIS datasets is essentially the same as one group in an hierarchical dataset, and so our
hierarchical dataset contains three groups. Likewise, the dictionary file
from the hierarchical dataset describes the variables in each of the
groups. The logical structure of this hierarchical dataset, (often
referred to as a schema) can be illustrated as in Figure 8-1.

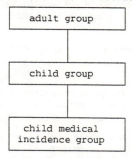

Fig. 8-1. Schema Example

93

The schema is a diagrammatic representation of a particular structural relationship of the groups in the dataset. In OSIRIS this schema must take the form of a hierarchy, an overall logical structure in which each group except for the first is subordinate to a single group and each group may have none, one, or more than one group subordinate to it.[11] A hierarchical relationship is a one-to-many relationship in which every subordinate group belongs to one and only one higher group.

A Structure Definition Language (SDL) is used to describe the schema. In this language the user states which portions of the original standard OSIRIS datasets form groups in the hierarchical dataset. This language also describes the hierarchical relationship between the groups, and the specific variables which identify and link the groups in that hierarchy. The actual processing of these language statements and related datasets is done by the &SBUILD (or &UPDATE - see section 8.8) command, which produces the hierarchical dataset-- a data file and its corresponding dictionary.

The &SBUILD command puts all the dictionaries for all the groups together in one combined dictionary, and puts all the data together in one combined dataset. The result is a sequential file with data records of (potentially) different lengths for the different groups. In the dataset described by Figure 8-1, the first record is for an adult, followed immediately by the first child of that adult, if any. Then there are medical incident records for that child. Next comes the second child, with that child's medical incidents; then the third child; and so on until there are no more children or incidents associated with that adult. The next record is for the second adult, and so on. Figure 8-2 illustrates this structure.

Such datasets can be used directly as input to most OSIRIS commands by defining a specific subset of the hierarchical dataset. The subset has all of the characteristics of a standard (flat) OSIRIS dataset. No distinct file is actually generated. Instead, as the records are processed sequentially, an entry is built, and when completed it is passed directly to the calling command program. This entry is defined using the Entry Definition Language, (EDL). With this language the user may indicate which level becomes the unit of analysis for this run, which groups in the hierarchy are to be included in the entry, and how to handle multiple occurences of groups.

Sample entries are given in Figure 8-3. Here the Entry Definition Language was used to select the child as the unit of analysis, the adult was ignored, and space for up to two medical incidents was allocated. When there were fewer than two medical incidents per child, the missing variables were padded (depending on certain options) so that all of the entries have the same format.

Another example from the same dataset takes the medical incident as the unit of analysis, retaining both the child and adult groups. The resulting entries are shown in Figure 8-4.

Each use of the Entry Definition Language constitutes a statement of a specific logical subset of the original hierarchical dataset. The entries

---

[11]Commands to build and maintain network data structures are under development. It is expected that some of these commands, will be publicly available by Fall 1984. A network data structure is one that allows more or less arbitrarily complex relationships.

94

```
a.  Adult 1

b.  Adult 1's Child 1

c.  Adult 1's Child 1's Med.  Incid.  1

d.  Adult 1's Child 1's Med.  Incid.  2

e.  Adult 2

f.  Adult 3

g.  Adult 3's Child 1

h.  Adult 3's Child 1's Med.  Incid.  1

i.  Adult 3's Child 2

j.  Adult 3's Child 3

k.  Adult 3's Child 3's Med.  Incid.  1

l.  Adult 3's Child 3's Med.  Incid.  2

m.  Adult 3's Child 3's Med.  Incid.  3

n.  Adult 4
```

:
etc.

Fig. 8-2. Hierarchical Data File Example

Entry (Child)	Child	Medical Incident 1	Medical Incident 2
1	a. Adult 1's Child 1	b. Adult 1's Child 1' Medical Incident 1	c. Adult 1's Child 1's Medical Incident 2
2	g. Adult 3's Child 1	h. Adult 3's Child 1's Medical Incident 1	pad
3	i. Adult 3's Child 2	pad	pad
4	j. Adult 3's Child 3	k. Adult 3's Child 3's Medical Incident 1	l. Adult 3's Child 3's Medical Incident 2

Fig. 8-3. Hierarchical Entry Example (unit of analysis is child)

95

Entry (Medical Incident)	Adult	Child	Medical Incident
1	a. Adult 1	b. Adult 1's Child 1	c. Adult 1's Child 1's Medical Incident 1
2	a. Adult 1	b. Adult 1's Child 1	d. Adult 1's Child 1's Medical Incident 2
3	f. Adult 3	g. Adult 3's Child 1	h. Adult 3's Child 1's Medical Incident 1
4	f. Adult 3	j. Adult 3's Child 3	k. Adult 3's Child 3's Medical Incident 1
5	f. Adult 3	j. Adult 3's Child 3	l. Adult 3's Child 3's Medical Incident 2
6	f. Adult 3	j. Adult 3's Child 3	m. Adult 3's Child 3's Medical Incident 3

Fig. 8-4. Second Hierarchical Entry Example
(unit of analysis is medical incident)

that are delivered from an hierarchical dataset to an OSIRIS command
program look like flat data from any standard OSIRIS dataset. Hence all
the usual OSIRIS functions such as filtering to select cases, recoding of
variables, and so on, may be performed on the retrieved data.

8.3 When to Use Structured Files

The following points should be kept in mind when deciding whether or not
to build a hierarchical structured file.

(i) Only hierarchical data structures can be used: network
structures must be simplified into hierarchies.[12]

(ii) A structured file may reduce the total size of data files
by eliminating unnecessary padding. However users should
note that a structured data file adds a certain amount of

---

[12]See footnote page 94.

information to link and sequence the data records.
There is also some processing overhead on the computer to
handle the file structure and create entries for analysis.
The exact point at which it will prove more efficient to
create a structured dataset rather than a padded
standard OSIRIS dataset is difficult to determine, but as a
rough guide the user may find the hierarchical capability is of no
advantage if the padding that can be removed from an standard
OSIRIS dataset consumes less than 25 percent of the total
file.

(iii) A structured file allows the user to alter the data
structure from one analysis run to another, e.g., by
changing the unit of analysis and realigning other portions of
the data structure to it.

8.4   A Hypothetical Hierarchical Dataset

We shall use a small hypothetical hierarchical dataset for the examples
in this chapter.

Suppose we had the following three standard OSIRIS datasets:

A dataset for eight states

    V1   State ID   –Unique (1-8)
    V2   Region
    V3   State Size

A dataset for twenty cities

    V1   State ID   –Link
    V2   City ID   –Unique (1-20)
    V3   Type of City Government
    V4   City Size

A dataset for fifty respondents

    V1   State ID   –Link
    V2   City ID   –Link
    V3   Respondents ID   –Unique (1-50)
    V4   Satisfaction With State Government
    V5   Satisfaction With City Government
    V6   Satisfaction With Transportation

In the lists above, the identification, or link, variables have been
noted for each group. These variables are necessary to link each group to
those above it in the structure. In general, for each dataset, there
should be

        (i)   a unique ID

        (ii) links to datasets above it in the hierarchy

OSIRIS dictionaries and data for these (made-up) datasets are shown in Appendix D.[13]

The natural way to organize these three datasets is

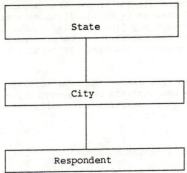

Fig. 8.5. Schema for Hypothetical Data

Usually a single group or <u>root</u> is selected for the top level of the hierarchy. One or more groups may be linked to this root, forming the second level. Additional groups may be linked to those of the second level, and these form a still lower, third level, and so on down the tree.

In the simple example above we have only one group per level. But we could, for example, have had a second dataset of, say, State Senators, at Level 2. Typically there is a single group at Level 1, but there may be more than one. The OHDS manual, Appendix B, gives an example of multiple groups at Level 1.

8.5   Creating a Structured File: The &SBUILD Command

The &SBUILD setup used to create a structured dataset from the hypothetical data is shown below.

```
$RUN   ISR:OSIRIS.IV
&SBUILD    DICTIN1=DISTA DICTIN2=DICIT DICTIN3=DIRES   -
DATAIN1=DASTA DATAIN2=DACIT DATAIN3=DARES    -
DICTOUT=DISTRUCT DATAOUT=DASTRUCT DATATEMP=-T
MY STRUCTURED FILE                             Label
PR=OUTDICT                                     Parameter Stmt.
GNUM=1 LEVEL=1 V=ALL NAME='STATE GROUP' INFI=IN1  Struc. Defin. Stmts.
GNUM=2 LEVEL=2 V=ALL RENU=V101 NAME='CITY GROUP' INFI=IN2 -
LINK=(G1.V1:G2.V1)
GNUM=3 LEVEL=3 V=ALL RENU=V201 NAME='RESP GROUP' INFI=IN3  -
ID=3 LINK=(G3.V2:G2.V2,G3.V1:G1.V1)
&END
```

---

[13](They are also publicly available on University of Michigan account (CCID) SDM3; they may be read or copied from that number. The files are named DISTA, DASTA, DICIT, DACIT, DIRES, and DARES. See also DISTRUCT and DASTRUCT.

&SBUILD expects to receive statements in the following order:

1 - input and output filename assignments
      (including a temporary file, DATATEMP, needed by the
      command)[14]
2 - filter statements - optional
3 - label statement
4 - parameter statement
5 - structure definition statements
6 - END statement -conditional (use if giving Entry Defini-
      tion)
7 - default Entry Definition -optional
8 - &END

When planning a setup, the first important matter to be considered is
the order in which the groups are described. With your schema in front of
you, start by describing the group at the root. Then follow the branch to
the left and down to the second level and describe that group. Continue to
the left and down: describe the left-most group at the third level.
Repeat, moving to the left and down, until you reach the "leaf" at the end
of the branch. At this point, return up the branch you followed until you
find a group (node) which branches down again. Follow the branch down,
describing the second group from the left (since the left-most group has
already been described). Continue down and left as before. If you were
tracing the trees with a pencil, the idea is to keep to the left and go to
the bottom, always finding untouched groups at nodes before moving back up
the tree or to the right. The tree in Fig. 8-6 is numbered in the sequence
in which groups should be described to &SBUILD, if we were to describe a
dataset with 17 groups and 5 levels.

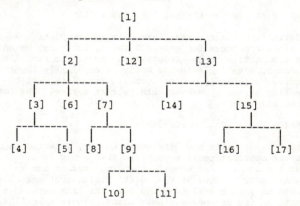

Fig. 8.6. The Order in Which Groups Should be Specified to &SBUILD

The Structure Definition Statements (item 5 on the list above) are the
heart of an &SBUILD setup. Each Structure Definition Statement is made up
of keywords selected from the following list:

---

[14]If the structured datafile is large a file of the appropriate size should
be explicitly created before OSIRIS is run.

```
DUP      IDVARS   RECODE
END      INFILE   RENUMBER
ENTRY    LEVEL    REPETITIONS
FILTER   LINK     VARS
GNUM     NAME
```

Starting with the group at the root in our schema, we assign a group number to be used for later reference, a descriptive name, and the corresponding level number identifying to which level in the hierarchy the group belongs. The root is at LEVEL=1 and is usually the only group at that level. At any other level there is often more than one group.

        GNUM=1 NAME='STATE GROUP' LEVEL=1

We can also add the suffix which will be appended to "DICT" and "DATA" to set the input and output names that will be used on the left of the equals sign when assigning the input dictionary and dataset for this group:

        GNUM=1 NAME='STATE GROUP' LEVEL=1 INFILE=IN1

Next we decide which of the variables from the household file are to be included in the household group. There are various ways to specify variables using the VARS keyword.

Since we want all of the input varibles we can specify:

        VARS=ALL

The structure definition statement now looks like this:

        GNUM=1 NAME='STATE GROUP' LEVEL=1 INFI=IN1 V=ALL

The structure definition for the state group is now complete. We are now ready to do a similar process for groups 2 and 3, but first we must consider how these groups link to the group at the root. To establish a link between two groups, a variable in one group is explicitly identified with the corresponding variable in another group. Each link must be described with the LINK keyword, one variable pair at a time. The format for the LINK keyword is:

        LINK=(Gn.Vm:Ga.Vb,...,Gn'.Vm':Ga'.Vb')

To specify a given link, write down the group number, a period, and the variable number of the appropriate link point in that group (e.g. G5.V342). Then add a colon (:) and specify the group number and variable of the other group as before. Thus G5.V342:G4.V1 states that variable V342 in group G5 is linked to variable V1 in group G4. The link between a pair of groups may consist of one or more variable pairs. These specifications should be written from left to right in the appropriate sort order, with primary sort variables preceding secondary sort variables.

For each leaf group after the first we must define the variables which link the group to the ones above it in the structure. Thus the link between the City group and the State group is the State Identification variable. This variable exists in both the State and the City input datasets and can be matched when creating the hierarchy; thus the link is G2.V1:G1.V1. The link between the Respondent group and the City group is the City identification variable, G3.V2:G2.V2. For efficient execution of

&SBUILD one should specify not only the link between any given group and the one at the next higher level, but also the links from that group to groups at all higher levels on the same branch. The link between the Respondents group and the State group is G3.V1:G1.V1.

For each leaf group we must also define an identification variable using the IDVARS keyword. An identification variable is a quasi-link variable: it is the variable that would be the link variable if the group had a subordinate group. In our example, the Respondent identification number is the identification variable.

The main body of the &SBUILD setup example is now complete. The next step is to define the input and output filenames on the &command line. Each of the files to be used as input must be defined using the names "DICTxxxx" and "DATAxxxx" where "xxxx" is a 1-4 character suffix supplied by the INFILE keyword. Thus if INFILE=IN1, as for the state group, the input dataset will be defined using DICTIN1 and DATAIN1. An example of this is:

```
       &SBUILD DICTIN1=DISTA DATAIN1=DASTA -
               DICTIN2=DICIT DATAIN2=DACIT -
               DICTIN3=DIRES DATAIN3=DARES -
               DICTOUT=DISTRUCT DATAOUT=DASTRUCT -
               DATATEMP=-T
```

Next insert a descriptive label for the printed output. A parameter statement follows the label, to define the parameter options. Then the all important structure definition statements. (After the Structure Definition Statements we may optionally enter a Default Entry Definition to be used later for flat file retrieval in case no other Entry Definition is given by the user. A Default Entry Definition can be useful if the structured dataset is going to be accessed in the same way nearly all of the time. That was not done in our example.)

Although the above example is almost deceptively simple, it serves as an introduction to structured files. A more complicated example is given in the OHDS Manual; in the course of working through that example additional keywords are explained and exercised.

8.6 Accessing a Structured File: The &ENTRY Command

An OSIRIS hierarchical dataset to be used in an OSIRIS command setup can be reorganized for retrieval in different ways using the Entry Definition Language. EDL is used to define an entry from one or more physical input records from the structured dataset. As many input records as are necessary to fulfill the requirements described in the Entry Definition will be read before the appropriate collection of data is passed on as an entry to the calling command program. This entry will then be treated as though it were a single record from a flat file.

The following is a list of possible keywords to be used in the EDL:

ENTRY	MAXOCC	REPETITIONS
GNUM	OPT	UNIT
Gn...	RENUMBER	VINCR
LEVEL		

The entry definition is given in an &ENTRY command, preceding other &COMMANDS the setup. The user may also have created a Default Entry Definition in the dictionary, which will be used if no Entry Definitions are present in the setup. The &ENTRY command processes the EDL for syntax errors and passes it on to the subsequent command program which then executes the EDL, contructing and using the entries one at a time.

There are three different kinds of statements in the Entry Definition Language: a parameter statement, an inter-group logical definition, and one or more group definitions.

The order in which statements should be entered is:

    1 - &command statement
    2 - parameter statement
    3 - inter-group logical definition
    4 - group definitions

The parameter statement provides the identification number for the entry (more than one can be defined) and the level number of the unit of analysis chosen using the keywords ENTRY and UNIT respectively. With three different levels in the example schema we could select the State as the unit of analysis (UNIT=1), the City (UNIT=2), or the Respondent (UNIT=3). The UNIT keyword tells the &ENTRY command when it must check for a complete entry. In other words, with the following parameter statement,

ENTRY=1 UNIT=1

records will be read from the input file and data will be accumulated in the entry until the next State record is encountered. The &ENTRY command will then check to see if it has a valid entry according to the parameters supplied in the inter-group logical definition and the group definitions. If the entry is valid, it will be passed on to the calling command program; if not, the &ENTRY command starts again to build an entry based on the new State record.

In the inter-group logical definition we describe the combination of groups which make up the entry. We may be interested in data from a single group only (such as all of the Cities in our study) or in a combination of groups. We might require the presence of all three groups to make an entry, so that

ENTRY=1 UNIT=1
G1 + G2 + G3

would select only those City States which contain at least one City and at least one Respondent for that City. In this example, data from all three groups would be included in the entry created. The entry itself would look like this:

G1	G2	G3

An Entry Definition may be complete when it contains only the parameter statement and the inter-group logical definition, without any group defini- tions at all. It is important to note, however, that great care must be taken so that the entry created makes logical sense. The Entry Definition given above makes sense for an input file which contains a single City and a single Respondent per state as shown in Figure 8.7.

record number	group number	data records
1	1	State 1
2	2	State 1's City
3	3	State 1's City Respondent
4	1	State 2
5	2	State 2's City
6	3	State 2's City Respondent
7	1	State 3
8	2	State 3's City
9	3	State 3's City Respondent
:	:	:
:	:	:

Fig. 8-7.   EDL File Example 1.

It may not be appropriate, however, for an input file which contains more than one City and/or Respondent for each State, in which the user may want to examine the data for the additional Cities and/or Respondents as well. (See Figure 8-8.) In this case the G1+G2+G3 example would result in entries containing only the information related to the last City in the State and the last Respondent for that City.

record number	group number	data records		
1	1	State 1		
2	2	State 1's	City 1	
3	2	State 1's	City 2	
4	3	State 1's	City 2's	Respondent 1
5	3	State 1's	City 2's	Respondent 2
6	2	State 1's	City 3	
7	2	State 1's	City 4	
8	1	State 2		
:	:	:		
:	:	:		

Fig. 8-8.   EDL File Example 2.

There are several ways to make clear in the Entry Definition just which occurences of each group are to be retrieved. One way is to add the group definition statements to clarify the structure of the entry. Another way would be to change the unit of analysis. A level 2 unit of analysis, UNIT=2, in this case would give us an entry for each City who had an as- sociated respondent (but only the last Respondent for that City), and UNIT=3 gives us an entry for each respondent.

In the group definitions, we specify certain options that apply only to a particular group given in the inter-group logical definition. the group number is specified with the GNUM keyword. With the OPT keyword, for ex-

103

ample, a group may be defined as optional, that is we can allow a valid entry to be made even if the data for the group is missing. This means that the group in the inter-group logical definition will always be treated as "true" or present even if it is not.

```
ENTRY=2 UNIT=1
G1+G2+G3
GNUM=2 OPT
```

This Entry Definition would return an entry for all States with an associated Respondent whether or not any City record was given. (The city variables would be padded according to the NODATA keyword on the program parameter statement.)

The MAXOCC= and VINCR= keywords allow for multiple occurances. MAXOCC stands for maximum occurences and VINCR for variable number increment; the latter keyword is used to avoid duplicate variable numbers. When retrieving multiple occurrences of a group the LEVEL= keyword must be used to temporarily raise the level of a group. For example, City might be raised to State level so that the City records an be grouped together. Here is an entry at the State level with up to ten Cities:

S	C1	C2	C3	C4	C5	C6	C7	C8	C9	C10
G1	G2	G2	G2	G2	G2	G2	G2	G2	G2	G2

```
ENTRY=1   UNIT=1
G1+G2
GNUM=2 OPT LEVEL=1 MAXOCC=10 VINCR=100
```

It is also possible to retrieve multiple groups at the same level. this might be useful if one had a structure such as the one shown below.

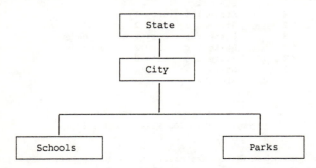

Further examples of using the Entry Definition Language to access our structured dataset are:

(1) To retrieve an entry for every Respondent, along with the City and State data:

```
ENTRY=1 UNIT=3
G1+G2+G3
```

(2) To retrieve an entry for each State and one City, regardless of whether or not there was an associated City:

```
ENTRY=2 UNIT=1
G1+G2
GNUM=2 OPTIONAL LEVEL=1
```

(3) To retrieve an entry for every State and up to ten Respondents per State

```
ENTRY=3 UNIT=1
G1+G3
GNUM=3 OPT LEVEL=1 MAXOCC=10 VINCR=100
```

8.7 Using &ENTRY in A Command Setup

Suppose we wanted to list all the respondents, along with their City and State data. We would use the &ENTRY command to define the appropriate Entry Definition. In the command setup - here an &DSLIST - we would give the ENTRY keyword on the parameter statement.

```
&ENTRY
ENTRY=7 UNIT=3                   Global Definition
G1+G2+G3                         Inter-group Definition
GNUM=1 OPT                       Group Definitions
GNUM=2 OPT
&END
&DSLIST DICTIN=DISTRUCT DATAIN=DASTRUCT
LISTING OF ALL RESPONDENTS      Label
V=ALL ENTRY=7                    DSLIST Para. Stmt. Note ENTRY keyword
&END
```

8.8 Additional Commands for Hierarchical Datasets

The OSIRIS &UPDATE command can be used in much the same manner as &SBUILD to build a structured dataset. In addition, &UPDATE has the capability to update an existing structured dataset; it can add, delete, or replace groups, occurences, or variables in a structured dataset. (&UPDATE can also be used on ordinary flat files; for example, in section 5.6 it was used to merge two files.)

The &DICT and &FCOR commands can be used to correct dictionaries or data for hierarchical files. The &TRANS command can be used to create a rectangular dataset from a hierarchical dataset. &SENTRY is a command to transform a non-OSIRIS hierarchically structured dataset into an OSIRIS hierarchical dataset.

8.9 Some Recommendations

If you plan to build a structured file, it is a good idea to try a few schemas, sketch some tree diagrams, and set up the Entry Definition Language needed to retrieve the desired data. Once a plan is made it is high-ly recommended that you build a sample dataset containing all of the groups in the selected schema. Enough data should be included to represent all

105

possible combinations of groups being either present or missing, or containing multiple occurences, but not so much as to be costly and time consuming to use. Various Entry Definitions can be tried on the sample dataset, and the entries so created should be examined carefully. When you are satisfied that the schema is correct, the full hierarchical dataset may be built. The sample dataset can be kept available so it is possible to test any new Entry Definitions you may wish to try at a later date.

EPILOGUE

What we attempt in this manual is an explanation of rationales behind the functions and special features of certain important programs within the OSIRIS package. The user may, at first, be overwhelmed by the lists of things to watch for, the exceptions to rules and so forth. The user should realize that standardized features of OSIRIS are equally, if not more, important to learn. These standarized features of the OSIRIS system are explained within this manual but are not repeated within each program description. Thus, they may be forgotten or overlooked in the rush to become familiar with rule exceptions.

These standard features are emphasized within the OSIRIS IV Manual [10] where each program and setup is explained in detail and examples are presented. In the OSIRIS Manual each program option and requirement is documented. The user should refer to the OSIRIS Manual when actually setting up runs for OSIRIS programs. Over time, its standardized format will become familiar to the user and the common features shared by OSIRIS programs will become obvious.

We hope that this manual will be useful as an introduction to data processing in the social sciences and as supplemental source of information about OSIRIS programs. Initially, the program descriptions should aid the user in understanding basic data processing principles and in planning an appropriate processing sequence. Later, as the OSIRIS user becomes more proficient, this manual will be unnecessary: the user will find that he has graduated to the OSIRIS IV Manual.

REFERENCES

[1]   Bixby, T. G., Brevoort, S. L., and Marks, G. A. OHDS An
        Introduction to OSIRIS Hierarchical Data Structures. Ann Arbor:
        Inter-University Consortium for Political and Social Research,
        Center for Political Studies, Institute for Social Research,
        University of Michigan, 1979.

[2]   [BMDP] Dixon, W. J., editor. BMDP Statisical Software.
        Revised. Berkeley, California: University of California Press,
        1983.

[3]   Clubb, J. M. and Traugott, M. W. Using Computers. Washington:
        Division of Educational Affairs The American Political Science
        Association, 1978.

[4]   [Utility-Coder] Documentation Department of Cambridge Computer
        Associates. User's Manual for Utility-Coder. Third edition.
        Cambridge, Massachusetts: Cambridge Computer Associates, 1977 .

[5]   IBM System/360 and System/370 FORTRAN IV Language. GC28-6515.

[6]   IBM System/360 and System/370 Operating System Messages and Codes.
        GC28-6631.

[7]   [MIDAS] Fox, D. J., and Guire, K. E. Documentation for MIDAS
        Third edition. Ann Arbor: Statistical Research Laboratory, The
        University of Michigan, 1976.

[8]   [MTS] The University of Michigan Computing Center Staff.
        Introductory Guides. Ann Arbor: The University of Michigan
        Computing Center. The following four introductions are the most
        useful for the OSIRIS user.

        a) Introduction to the Computing Center, September 1983.
        b) Introduction to Magnetic Tapes, January 1982.
        c) Introduction to MTS, January 1984.
        d) Introduction to Terminals, September 1983.

[9]   [MTS] The University of Michigan Computing Center Staff.
        MTS Manual. Ann Arbor: The University of Michigan Computing Center.

        The following volumes are particularly useful for the general user.

        a) Volume One: "The Michigan Terminal System," January
            1984.
        b) Volume Two: "Public File Descriptions," April 1982.
            Updates 1 and 2 must be applied to this edition.
        c) Volume Four: "Terminals in MTS," March 1984.
        d) Volume Nineteen: "Tapes and Floppy Disks,"
            February 1983.

[10]   [OSIRIS] Survey Research Center Computer Support Group. OSIRIS
        IV User's Manual. Seventh edition. Revised. Ann Arbor: Institute
        for Social Research, The University of Michigan, 1982.

[11]   [SAS] SAS Institute, Inc. SAS User's Guide: Basics, 1982 edition.
        Raleigh, North Carolina: SAS Institute, 1982.

[12]   [SAS] SAS Institute, Inc. <u>The SAS Supplemental Library User's</u>
        <u>Guide</u>, 1980 edition. Cary, North Carolina: SAS Institute, 1980.

[13]   [SPSS] Nie, N. H., Hull, C. H., Jenkins, J.G.G., Steinbrenner,
        K., and Bent, D. H. <u>SPSS Statistical Package for the Social</u>
        <u>Sciences</u>. Second edition. New York: McGraw-Hill, 1975.

[14]   [SPSS] Hull, C. H., and Nie, H. H. SPSS update 7-9: <u>New</u>
        <u>Procedures and Facilities for Releases 7-9</u>. New York:
        McGraw-Hill, 1981.

[15]   [SPSS^x] Spss Inc. <u>SPSS^x User's Guide</u>. New York:
        McGraw-Hill, 1983.

[16]   Weisberg, H. F. and Bowen, B. D. <u>An Introduction to Survey</u>
        <u>Research and Data</u>. San Francisco: W. H. Freeman and company ,
        1977.

QUESTIONNAIRES AND CODEBOOKS

A.1 Campus Unrest Questionnaire

Study 400   INTERVIEWER:_____

CAMPUS UNREST - QUESTIONNAIRE

1) State   _____

2) Respondent identification   _____

3) How old are you?   _____
                                                      (in years)

4) Are you married, single, widowed, divorced or separated?

    __ 1 Married   __ 2 Single   __ 3 Widowed, Divorced or Separated

5) How many grades of school did you finish? _____
                                                        (grade)

6) Next we would like to ask you about your work. Are you working now, or
    unemployed?

    _____ 1 Employed

    _____ 2 Unemployed ------> Go to Q8

7) What is your main occupation - that is, what kind of work do you do to
    earn a livelihood?

    _____
         [INTERVIEWER: If not clear:]
    Tell me a little more about what you do

    _____

         [INTERVIEWER: Ask only if respondent is married (1 on Q4) and
                        respondent is a female]

8) What is your husband's occupation?

    _____

    _____

[15]Remember that the Campus Unrest data are simulated - they were generated
by a computer. There never was a real questionnaire or a real codebook.
The "questionnaire" and "codebook" in this Appendix are presented only to
aid in following the computer processing examples in the text. They should
not be taken as models!

9) What is or was your father's occupation?

_____

[INTERVIEWER: Substitute name of nearest city of population
greater than 50,000]

10) How long does it take you to get to (nearest city)? _____

11) How often do you read each of the following newspapers?

	More than once a week (1)	Less than once a week (2)	Never (3)
a) New York Times	____	____	____
b) Ann Arbor News	____	____	____
c) Detroit Free Press	____	____	____
d) Wall Street Journal	____	____	____
e) Christian Science Monitor	____	____	____
f) Daily Worker	____	____	____
g) Washington Post	____	____	____

12) Do you have children in college or soon to go (within the next 2
years)?

____ 1 No children

____ 2 Children, but in elementary school

____ 3 Soon to go

____ 4 In college

13) Did you do any work for either of the political parties during the
November 1968 election?

____ 1 No work

____ 2 Sought people to sign petitions

____ 3 Sought people to sign petitions and other activities

14) Students claim that they wany more of a voice than they now have in
choosing faculty, in curriculum and the like. Do you feel they have
enough of a voice now or do you think they should have more of a
voice?

____ 1 Have too much voice now ____ 2 Enough ____ 3 More

15) Some people claim that student demonstrations are part of a nation-wide conspiracy - perhaps Communist led. How do you feel about this?

_____ 1 Not conspiracy

_____ 2 Conspiracy, not Communist led

_____ 3 Conspiracy, Communist led

16) Some people feel that universities should ban organizations such as SDS. Do you agree or disagree?

_____ 1 Disagree   _____ 2 Agree

17) Some people claim that we should get out of Viet Nam immediately. Others feel that we ought to slowly end the fighting and to slowly remove our troops. Still others feel that we ought to continue fighting and see the war to a successful victory. How do you feel?

_____ 1 Continue fighting

_____ 2 Withdraw slowly

_____ 3 Withdraw immediately

18) Some people say that in spite of what people say, the lot of the average man is getting worse. Do you disagree or agree?

_____ 1 Disagree   _____ 2 Agree

19) It's hardly fair to bring children into the world the way things look for the future. Do you disagree or agree?

_____ 1 Disagree   _____ 2 Agree

20) These days a person doesn't really know who he can count on. Do you disagree or agree?

_____ 1 Disagree   _____ 2 Agree

21) Nowadays a person has to live pretty much for today and let tomorrow take care of itself. Do you disagree or agree?

_____ 1 Disagree   _____ 2 Agree

Observation Data

(INTERVIEWER: BY OBSERVATION ONLY)

22) Number of calls: _____ (Give number)

23) Sex: _____ 1 Male   _____ 2 Female

24) Race: _____ 1 White   _____ 2 Black   _____ 3 Other, Specify
_____

25) Respondent's town or nearest city of population 50,000
_____

113

26) Number of miles from respondent's home to city given above (Q25)
_____

27) Size of respondent's community _____
      (If population under 100, write rural)

A.2. Example of Part of a Precoded Questionnaire

PART A.

This part of the questionnaire asks you to describe the kind of person you are. Please read each sentence, then mark the box that shows how often it is true for you:

KEY:

(1)=ALMOST ALWAYS TRUE
(2)=OFTEN TRUE
(3)=SOMETIMES TRUE
(4)=SELDOM TRUE
(5)=NEVER TRUE

(CHECK ONE BOX ON EACH LINE)

card column			(1)	(2)	(3)	(4)	(5)
(1:16)	1.	I am a useful guy to have around	—	—	—	—	—
(1:17)	2.	I demand freedom and independence above everything	—	—	—	—	—
(1:18)	3.	When I have mastered something, I look for opportunities to do it	—	—	—	—	—
(1:19)	4.	I complain about my sufferings and hardships	—	—	—	—	—
(1:20)	5.	I feel that I'm a person of worth, at least on an equal plane with others	—	—	—	—	—
(1:21)	6.	I get angry and smash things	—	—	—	—	—
(1:22)	7.	I try to stay out of situations where I don't see any chance for progress or advancement	—	—	—	—	—
(1:23)	8.	I am discouraged when things go wrong	—	—	—	—	—
(1:24)	9.	I feel that I have a number of good qualities	—	—	—	—	—
(1:25)	10.	I become stubborn when others try to force me to do something	—	—	—	—	—
(1:26)	11.	When I have a problem, I try to get help from others	—	—	—	—	—
(1:27)	12.	When the work I'm doing doesn't give me the chance to do the things I'm good at, I am dissatisfied	—	—	—	—	—
(1:28)	13.	I feel that I can't do anything right	—	—	—	—	—
(1:29)	14.	I like to be on my own and be my own boss	—	—	—	—	—
(1:30)	15.	As a person I do a good job these days	—	—	—	—	—

Variable number	Card 10 Column Number		
	1-4	Respondent sequence number - 4 digits. No missing data	
	5-6	Card (deck) number Code 10	
1	7-8	Q1	State 1 Michigan 2 Arizona 3 California 4 North Carolina 5 New York
3	9	Q22	Number of calls 0 Missing Data 1 One 2 Two 3 Three or More
2	10-11	Q2	Respondent identification 2 digits. No missing data
4	12 Code 00 in col. 23-24	Q23	Sex 1 Male 2 Female
5	13	Q24	Race 0 Missing 1 White 2 Black
	Make a Card		3 Other
6	14	Q4	Marital Status 0 Missing data 1 Married 2 Single 3 Widowed, Divorced, Separated

---

[16]   The term "preliminary codebook" is used to describe the codebook used during coding, keypunching and preliminary data processing. This codebook locates the original data on 80 column cards or card images. Within its pages, each variable is identified verbally, its codes are presented and its card and column locations are provided.

After the data are keypunched and written onto magnetic tape or disk this same codebook may be used to locate data as long as they are in card image format.

7	15-16	Q3	Age of Respondent

7   15-16   Q3 Age of Respondent
0-97   Code actual age in years
  98   Age 98 or over
  99   Missing data

8   17   Q5 Education

0	Missing data	6	9 grades
1	0-4 grades	7	10 grades
2	5 grades	8	11 grades
3	6 grades	9	12 grades
4	7 grades	&	13-15 grades
5	8 grades		(some college)
		-	16 or more grades (college degree)

9   18-19   Q7 Occupation

0	Missing data	8	Labourer
1	Professional	9	Farmer, farm labourer
2	Manager		
3	Sales	10	Student
4	Clerical	11	Retired
5	Craftsman, foreman	12	On welfare
		13	Housewife
6	Operative	14	No Occupation
7	Service worker		

10   20   Q6 Employment status

0 Missing data
1 Employed
2 Unemployed

24   21   Q27 Size of community of respondént

0	Missing data	5	50,000-99,000
1	Over 1,000,000	6	25,000-49,999
2	500,000-999,999	7	10,000-24,999
3	250,000-499,999	8	Under 10,000
4	100,000-249,999	9	Rural

11   22   Q9 Father's occupation

0	Missing data	5	Craftsman, foreman
1	Professional		
2	Manager	6	Operative
3	Sales	7	Service Worker
4	Clerical	8	Labourer
		9	Farmer, farm labourer

12	23-24	Q8	Husband's occupation

Q8 Husband's occupation

0 Missing data	8 Labourer
1 Professional	9 Farmer, farm
2 Manager	labourer
3 Sales	10 Student
4 Clerical	11 Retired
5 Craftsman,	12 On welfare
foreman	13 Permanently
6 Operative	disabled
7 Service worker	14 No Occupation

13   25   Q12 Children in college
0 Missing data
1 No Children
2 Children but in elementary school
3 Soon to go to college
4 In college

14   26   Q13 Work for political parties in
1968 elections
0 Missing data
1 No work
2 Sought people to sign petitions
3 Sought people to sign petitions and
other activities

15   27   Q14 Student voice
0 Missing data
1 Have too much now
2 Have enough
3 Need more

16   28   Q15 Conspiracy
0 Missing data
1 Not conspiracy
2 Conspirary - Not Communist led
3 Conspiracy - Communist led

17   29   Q16 Ban SDS
0 Missing Data
1 Disagree
2 Agree

18   30   Q17 Viet Nam
0 Missing data
1 Continue fighting
2 Withdraw slowly
3 Withdraw immediately

19   31   Q18 Lot of average man
0 Missing data
1 Disagree
2 Agree

20	32	Q19 Children into world
		0 Missing data
		1 Disagree
		2 Agree

21	33	Q20 Count on people
		0 Missing data
		1 Disagree
		2 Agree

22	34	Q21 Live for today
		0 Missing data
		1 Disagree
		2 Agree

| | 78-80 | Study number |
| | | Code 400 |

Variable number	Card 12 Column Number	
	5-6	Card (deck) number code 12
	7-8	Q1 State Code
		1 Michigan
		2 Arizona
		3 California
		4 North Carolina
		5 New York
	10-11	Q2 Respondent identification 2 digits, no missing data
23	12-31	Q25 Respondent's nearest city or town Up to 20 letters left justified Leave blank if missing data.
25	32-34	Q26 Distance from nearest city Code miles in 3 digits 999-missing data
26	35-37	Q10 Travel time to nearest city Code in hours with one decimal place 999-missing data

```
27-33          40-46          Q11  Newspaper reading
                                   Use one column to code one
                                   newspaper.

                                   Code for frequency of reading
                                   newspapers:
                                   1  More than once a week
                                   2  Less than once a week
                                   3  Never
                                   9  Missing data

                                   Key to columns:
                                   40  New York Times
                                   41  Ann Arbor News
                                   42  Detroit Free Press
                                   43  Wall Street Journal
                                   44  Christian Science Monitor
                                   45  Daily Worker
                                   46  Washington Post

               78-80          Study number
                              Code 400
```

Appendix B

SAMPLE SETUPS FOR CAMPUS UNREST
DATA PROCESSING

```
$SIGNON SDM3              B.1 SETUP: BATCH JOB TO COPY CARDS TO DISK
MURPY
$CRE CUDATA SIZE=4P
$COPY *SOURCE* CUDATA
             .
             .       (CARD DATA)
             .
$ENDFILE
$LIST CUDATA
$SIGNOFF
```

```
$SIGNON SDM3              B.2 SETUP: SORT CUDATA
HELF
$CRE CUSORTED SIZE=4P
$RUN ISR:OSIRIS.IV
&COPYSORT SORTIN=CUDATA SORTOUT=CUSORTED -
S=CH,A,7,2,CH,A,10,2,CH,A,5,2 REC=200
$ENDFILE
$SIGNOFF
```

```
$SIGNON SDM3              B.3 SETUP: BATCH JOB TO CHECK THE COMPLETE-
SYB                                  NESS OF THE SORTED DATA
$CRE CUMERGED SIZE=4P
$RUN ISR:OSIRIS.IV
&MERCHECK DATAIN=CUSORTED DATAOUT=CUMERGED
CHECKING MERGE OF CAMPUS UNREST DATA
PRINT=ALL MAXP=2 IDCOL=(7-8,10-11) MAXE=20 DUPK=1 CONS='400' CLOC=78
DECK=10 IDLOC=5 PAD='-
     10II0II 0099000000000000000000000                                    40-
0'
DECK=12 IDLOC=5 PAD='-
     12II II                    999999  9999999                           40-
0'
$ENDFILE
$SIGNOFF
```

121

```
$SIGNON SDM3              B.4 SETUP: CREATE OSIRIS DICTIONARY
TESSA
$CRE MYDICT
$RUN ISR:OSIRIS.IV
&DICT DICTOUT=MYDICT
DICTIONARY FOR CAMPUS UNREST DATA
NREC=2 PRINT=(DI,OUTD)
V=1 NAME='STATE                   Q1'   WID=2 COL=7 RECO=1
V=2 NAME='RESPONDENT ID           Q2'   WID=2 COL=10
V=3 NAME='NUMBER OF CALLS         Q22'  WID=1 COL=9 MD1=0
V=4 NAME='SEX                     Q23'  WID=1 COL=12 MD1=NONE
V=5 NAME='RACE                    Q24'  WID=1 MD1=0
V=6 NAME='MARITAL STATUS          Q4'   WID=1 MD1=0
V=7 NAME='AGE                     Q3'   WID=2 MD1=99
V=8 NAME='EDUCATION               Q5'   WID=1 MD1=0 TY=A
V=9 NAME='OCCUPATION              Q7'   WID=2 MD1=0 TY=C
V=10 NAME='EMPLOYMENT STATUS      Q6'   WID=1 MD1=0
V=11 NAME='FATHER S OCCUPATION    Q9'   WID=1 MD1=0 COL=22
V=12 NAME='HUSBAND S OCC          Q8'   WID=2 MD1=0
V=13 NAME='CHILDREN IN COLLEGE    Q12'  WID=1 MD1=0
V=14 NAME='WORK FOR POL PARTY     Q13'  WID=1 MD1=0
V=15 NAME='STUDENT VOICE          Q14'  WID=1 MD1=0
V=16 NAME='CONSPIRACY             Q15'  WID=1 MD1=0
V=17 NAME='BAN SDS                Q16'  WID=1 MD1=0
V=18 NAME='VIET NAM               Q17'  WID=1 MD1=0
V=19 NAME='LOT OF AVERAGE MAN     Q18'  WID=1 MD1=0
V=20 NAME='CHILD INTO WORLD       Q19'  WID=1 MD1=0
V=21 NAME='COUNT ON PEOPLE        Q20'  WID=1 MD1=0
V=22 NAME='LIVE FOR TODAY         Q21'  WID=1 MD1=0
V=23 NAME='NEAREST LARGE CITY     Q25'  WID=20 TY=A COL=12 RECO=2
V=24 NAME='R S COMMUNITY SIZE     Q27'  WID=1 MD1=0 COL=21 RECO=1 TY=C
V=25 NAME='DIST FROM CITY         Q26'  WID=3 MD1=999 COL=32 RECO=2
V=26 NAME='TRAVEL TIME TO CITY    Q10'  WID=3 ND=1 MD1=99.9
V=27 NAME='NEW YORK TIMES         Q11'  WID=1 MD1=9 COL=40 ND=0
V=28 NAME='ANN ARBOR NEWS         Q11'  WID=1 MD1=9
V=29 NAME='DETROIT FREE PRESS     Q11'  WID=1 MD1=9
V=30 NAME='WALL STREET JOURNAL    Q11'  WID=1 MD1=9
V=31 NAME='CHRISTIAN SCIENCE MO   Q11'  WID=1 MD1=9
V=32 NAME='DAILY WORKER           Q11'  WID=1 MD1=9
V=33 NAME='WASHINGTON POST        Q11'  WID=1 MD1=9
$ENDFILE
$SIGNOFF
```

```
$SIGNON SDM3          B.5 SETUP: CORRECTING NON-NUMERIC CHARACTERS
JONAH                             IN CAMPUS UNREST DATA--THE &
$CRE NEWDICT
$CRE NEWDATA
$RUN ISR:OSIRIS.IV
&RECODE
 IF V8 EQ '0' THEN V8=0
 IF V8 EQ '1' THEN V8=1
 IF V8 EQ '2' THEN V8=2
 IF V8 EQ '3' THEN V8=3
```

```
IF V8 EQ '4' THEN V8=4
IF V8 EQ '5' THEN V8=5
IF V8 EQ '6' THEN V8=6
IF V8 EQ '7' THEN V8=7
IF V8 EQ '8' THEN V8=8
IF V8 EQ '9' THEN V8=9
IF V8 EQ '&' THEN V8=10
IF V8 EQ '-' THEN V8=11
&END
&TRANS DICTIN=MYDICT DATAIN=CUMERGED DICTOUT=NEWDICT DATAOUT=NEWDATA
RECODE AMPS AND DASHES.   REFORMAT TO ONE LOGICAL RECORD PER CASE.
R=1 V=1-33
V=8 WID=2 TYPE=C
$ENDFILE
$SIGNOFF




$SIGNON SDM3            B.6 SETUP: WILD CODE CHECKING
TENNIS
$RUN ISR:OSIRIS.IV
&WCC DICTIN=NEWDICT DATAIN=NEWDATA
CHECK WILD CODES
ID=(1,2,23)
V=3,5,6,18 CODES=0-3
V=4 CODES=1-2
V=12 MIN=0 MAX=14
V=17 CODES=0-2
V=1-2,7-11,13-16,19-33
$ENDFILE
$SIGNOFF




$SIGNON SDM3            B.7 SETUP: FILE CORRECTION
ORPHEUS
$CREATE DI4
$CREATE DA4
$RUN ISR:OSIRIS.IV
&FCOR DICTIN=NEWDICT DATAIN=NEWDATA DICTOUT=DI4 DATAOUT=DA4
EXCLUDE V1=5 AND V2=9 AND V7=47
RUN TO MAKE CORRECTIONS ON CAMPUS UNREST DATA
ID=1,2 PRINT=(DEL,CORR,DI)
ID=(1,7) V4=1,V12=0
ID=(2,1) V12=0
ID=(2,10) V11=1
ID=(3,5) V23=FRESNO,V25=000,V26=000,V27=3,V28=9,V30=3,V31=3,V32=3,V33=3
ID=(4,9) V5=1 V6=0
ID=(4,11) DEL
ID=(5,4) V18=3,V17=2
ID=(5,9) V3=1,V4=1,V5=1,V6=2,V7=47,V8=9 V10=1,V11=4,-
V12=0,V13=3,V14=1,V15=2,V16=2,V17=1,V18=1,V19=2,V20=1,V21=2,V22=1,-
V24=4,V25=999,V26=99.9
ID=(23,56) DEL
ID=(99,99) DEL
```

```
$ENDFILE
$SIGNOFF




$SIGNON SDM3              B.8 SETUP: CHECKING RECODE STATEMENTS
FANNY                           USING &DSLIST
$RUN ISR:OSIRIS.IV
&RECODE
 MDATA R16(0),R17(0)
 R16=BRAC(V16,3=1,2=2,1=3,ELSE=0)
 R17=BRAC(V17,2=1,1=3,ELSE=0)
 MDATA R100(0)
 R100=0
 R101=0
 IF NOT MDATA(V15) THEN R101=R101+1 AND R100=R100+V15
 IF NOT MDATA(R16) THEN R101=R101+1 AND R100=R100+R16
 IF NOT MDATA(R17) THEN R101=R101+1 AND R100=R100+R17
 IF NOT MDATA(V18) THEN R101=R101+1 AND R100=R100+V18
 IF R101 LT 2 THEN R100=0 ELSE R100=R100/R101
 NAME R100 'CONSERVATIVE INDEX'
&DSLIST DICTIN=DI4 DATAIN=DA4
CHECK THE INDEX
R=1 V=15-18,R16-R17,R100-R101 P=DI C=(1,50,5) SEQ
$ENDFILE
$SIGNOFF
```

SAMPLE PRINTOUTS FOR CAMPUS UNREST[1]
DATA PROCESSING

C.1 Printout: Copy Cards To Disk.
In this job, the data were
$LISTED after they were copied
to disk; listing is not practical
for large datasets.

This file, CUDATA is publicly
available on CCID SDM3 at the
University of Michigan.

```
$SIGNON SDM3 PRINTER=PAGE.ONESIDED COPIES=3   ROUTE=UNYN
Batch,Normal,Univ/Gov't
Last signon was at 16:51:52. Tue Jun 05/84
User SDM3 signed on at 17:07:59. Tue Jun 05/84


$CRE CUDATA SIZE=4P
File "CUDATA" has been created.

$COPY *SOURCE* CUDATA

$LIST CUDATA
```

125

[1] In certain cases material which appeared on two or more pages
has been consolidated by cut-and-paste.

```
Listing of CUDATA at 17:08:04 on JUN 5, 1984 for CCId=SDM3 Page    1

 1   12 1 3ANN ARBOR                    29 14   2323333          400
 2   9999999999                                                  400
 3                                                               400
 4   410 11 4211238.10214 01112122122        0   3322333        400
 5   12 1 4SAGINAW                                               400
 6   510 11 5212259 4114 0111212221 2   10   4   2112322        400
 7   12 1 5ANN ARBOR                     10   0   3333233        400
 8   13 1 5TRAVERSE CITY                  0   0                  400
 9   5 WRONG DECK                                                400
10   610 11 6112535 8198 0112111 1121        4   2112322        400
11   12 1 6ANN ARBOR                     10   4                  400
12   710 11 741372212257231 2221102 11    0   2211232           400
13   12.1 7DETROIT                         0                     400
14   810 11 8113757 5126 0121011221 1     0   2222213           400
15   12 1 8DETROIT                         0                     400
16   910 11 921240513211 1112022 2122      0   3232132          400
17   310 11 3212301 13277 71112212211      0                    400
18   12 1 9LANSING                                               400
19   1010 110112617 3193 01110111122       0   2333333          400
20   12 1 10GRAND RAPIDS                  45  12                 400
21   110 11 1212239 13294 73022212111                            400
22   123456789                                                  400
23   1110 22 1111246 12237B81132112121     0   1332313          400
24   12 2 1MESA                            0                     400
25   1210 21 2112177 10261 0112213212     130  25   2331233     400
26   12 2 2PHOENIX                                               400
27   1310 21 3212399 13243 3311222211      0   2333333          400
28   12 2 3TUCSON                          0                     400
29   1410 21 4212579 1165 0321201212      90  20   3333133      400
30   12 2 4PHOENIX                                               400
31   1510 21 5212156 13274 22102222212    60  20   3332233      400
32   12 2 5PHOENIX                                               400
33   1610 22 6112501 8116 0112221222       0   3331333          400
34   12 2 6LAS VEGAS                       0                     400
35   1710 22 71230- 1152 0112211212        0   3333333          400
36   12 2 7TUCSON                          0                     400
37   1810 21 8112269 6177 0212221212      38  10   2333333      400
38   12 2 8TEMPE                           0                     400
39   1910 21 9212439 4183 0100302211      55  15   1212213      400
40   12 2 1DETROIT                        162  35   2333333      400
41   2010 21102124 88 1191 04112121112    50  15                400
42   12 2 1OPHOENIX                                              400
43   2110 31 1212477 4194 0311221111       0   3333233          400
44   12 3 1SAN FRANCISCO                  105  28   2992323      400
45   2210 31 22137011226 8 0112201212      0                    400
46   12 3 2LOS ANGELES                     48  16   2993133      400
47   2310 31 3112541 5156 0311322211       0                    400
48   12 3 3SANTA BARBARA                   0   0   1993133       400
49   2410 31 4212369 13262 33112111220    25   8                400
50   12 3 4SAN FRANCISCO                   25   8   2992333      400
51   2510 31 51260- 1113 03222121222                            400
52   511111111111111111111111111111111111              400
53   10 3 5FRESNO                          0   0   3993333       400
54   210 12 2112827 11265 0111121121                            400
55   5222222222222222222222222222222222222222222222222  400
56   2610 32 6121291 8191 0112311210 1    68  24                400
57   12 3 6LOS ANGELES                     68  24   3991232      400
58   2710 31 7111225 10272 0113221211 21                        400

126
```

```
59   12 3   7LOS ANGELES              120 32   3992323   400
60  2810 31 8112585511272 01111110220           2993133   400
61   12 3   8SAN FRANCISCO            140 40   2993133   400
62  2910 31 9213731122 15 01211120020    0      2993313   400
63   12 3   9SANTA BARBARA             0         2993313   400
64  3010 3210222331 13237 62122212202    0      3992313   400
65   12 3  10SAN DIEGO                32 10     1321133   400
66   12 1   2KALAMAZOO 03212212202     0        1321133   400
67  3110 41 11228411 2235               0        3333333   400
68   12 4   1RALEIGH                   0         3333333   400
69  3210 41 2111171 2141 0112211 2222   0        2332132   400
70   12 4   2DURHAM                    0         2332132   400
71  3310 41 3212625 13282 3111112122             1332233   400
72   12 4   3WINSTON-SALEM            44 10     1332233   400
73  3410 41 4112631 7187 0311011 1111             2333331   400
74   12 4   4CHARLOTTE                72 25     2333331   400
75  3510 41 5112257 7157 0112322111     0        2331333   400
76   12 4   5RALEIGH                   0         2331333   400
77  3610 42 6212446 13241 2121112222     0       3333333   400
78   12 4   6RALEIGH                   0         3333333   400
79  3710 41 7299525 13291 2111111102     0       1333331   400
80   12 4   7GREENSBORO               81 22     1333331   400
81  3810 41 82112291 0213 0112223221 1            2332192   400
82   12 4   8DURHAM                    0         2332192   400
83  3910 41 9122409 1131 04321122122     0       2332222   400
84   12 4   9DURHAM                    0         2332222   400
85  4010 411101127661 11261 0101111122 2          1333233   400
86   12 4   1ORALEIGH                 160 35    1333233   400
87   21 4 11333333333333333333333333333333333333   400
88  4110 51 1112539 10274 0412112211 2            1322313   400
89   12 5   1NEW YORK                 46 20     1322313   400
90  4210 51 2212269 4195 0111222111 2             1331331   400
91   12 5   2ALBANY                   34  8     1331331   400
92  4310 51 311140 9 3194 0111200111 1            2332333   400
93   12 5   3BUFFALO                  30  6     2332333   400
94  4410 51 4123296 8176 0111334112 1             1331333   400
95   12 5   4ROCHESTER                56 12     1331333   400
96  4510 51 512279 3113 0212221212 2              2333322   400
97   12 5   5NEW YORK                  0         2333322   400
98  4610 51 611289 2171 0112211222 2              2331333   400
99   12 5   6NEW YORK                 40 12     2331333   400
100 4710 52 72121791 3293 3212212210              1333333   400
101  12 5   7ALBANY                   28  8     1333333   400
102 4810 51 8211706 12297 0120210111 8            2333333   400
103  12 5   8NEW YORK                 92 22     2333333   400
104  12 5   9SYRACUSE 01113211112      0         1332232   400
105 5010 5110112305 9199 0111321112               2333333   400
106  12 5  10NEW YORK                 36  7     2333333   400
107 4910051 912479 4144 0312211212 1              400
```

$SIGNOFF

C.2 Printout: &COPYSORT used to sort data.

Note that there is very little printout from &COPYSORT.

The OSIRIS Monitor prints the message of the day.

Check this line to see if job ran.

```
$SIGNON SDM3  PRINTER=PAGE,ONESIDED  COPIES=3 DELIVERY=ISR3 PAPER=PLAIN
Batch,Normal,Univ/Gov't
Last signon was at 16:45:24, Wed Jun 06/84
User SDM3 signed on at 12:58:19, Thu Jun 07/84


$CRE CUSORTED SIZE=4P
File "CUSORTED" has been created.


$RUN ISR:OSIRIS.IV
Execution begins   12:58:26


OSIRIS IV MONITOR SYSTEM
12:58:26 JUN 7, 1984
Issue 8NEWS for bulletins and Usage Tax notice.  Last changed 1/6/84.
&DCOR corrects directly structured datasets.  SRC/CSG has writeup.

&COPYSORT SORTIN=CUDATA SORTOUT=CUSORTED S=CH,A,7,2,CH,A,10,2,CH,A,5,2 REC=200
   107 RECORDS SORTED FROM SORTIN TO SORTOUT
RECORD LENGTH 80  INPUT BLKSIZE 80   OUTPUT BLOCK SIZE  80
***** Normal termination of COPYSORT $   0.04    0.06 secs


OSIRIS IV MONITOR SYSTEM
12:58:29 JUN 7, 1984

***** The last command has been processed.
Execution terminated   12:58:29  T=0.076  RC=0  $0.17


$SIGNOFF
```

```
$SIGNON SDM3  PRINTER=PAGE,ONESIDED  COPIES=3 DELIVERY=ISR3 PAPER=PLAIN
Batch,Normal,Univ/Gov't
Last signon was at 12:58:19, Thu Jun 07/84
User SDM3 signed on at 12:59:15. Thu Jun 07/84


$CRE CUMERGED SIZE=4P
File "CUMERGED" has been created.


$RUN ISR:OSIRIS.IV
Execution begins    12:59:21


OSIRIS IV MONITOR SYSTEM
12:59:21 JUN  7, 1984
Issue &NEWS for bulletins and Usage Tax notice.  Last changed 1/6/84.
&DCOR corrects directly structured datasets.  SRC/CSG has writeup.

&MERCHECK DATAIN=CUSORTED DATAOUT=CUMERGED
CHECKING MERGE OF CAMPUS UNREST DATA
PRINT=ALL MAXP=2 IDCOL=(7-8,10-11) MAXE=20 DUPK=1 CONS='400' CLOC=78
DECK=10 IDLOC=5 PAD='   10I10II 0099000000000000000000        400'
DECK=12 IDLOC=5 PAD='   12II II        999999    999999 9999999        400'
```

*** MERCHECK -- MERGE CHECKING PROGRAM ***

JUN 7, 1984   CHECKING MERGE OF CAMPUS UNREST DATA

CASE NUMBER   5   CASE ID 1 5
----
  1 EXTRA CARD(S) -- INVALID DECK NUMBER

GOOD RECORDS:
    510 11 5212259 4114 01112122212   0   0   3333233
     12 1 5TRAVERSE CITY

BAD RECORDS:
     13 1 5   WRONG DECK

"case number" is the program's count of sequential cases.

OK - &MERCHECK got the right record.

CASE NUMBER   6   CASE ID 1 6
----
     12 (2)
HAVE THE INDICATED NUMBER OF DUPLICATES

GOOD RECORDS:
    610 11 6112535 8198 0121211121
     12 1 6ANN ARBOR   10 4   2112322

BAD RECORDS:
     12 1 6ANN ARBOR   10 4   2112322

OK - &MERCHECK got the right record.

CASE NUMBER 25   CASE ID 3 5
----
     10 (2) 12 (2)
HAVE THE INDICATED NUMBER OF DUPLICATES

GOOD RECORDS:
   2510 31 511260- 1113 03222121222
     12 3 522222222222222222222222222222222222222

BAD RECORDS:
     10 3 5111111111111111111111111111111111
     12 3 5FRESNO   0 0   3993333

Here there were 2 10's and 2 12's. Program got the right 10 and the wrong 12. Deck 12 will have to be fixed.

CASE NUMBER 41   CASE ID 411
----
     1 EXTRA CARD(S) -- INVALID DECK NUMBER
DECKS:
  10   12
PADDED

BAD RECORDS:
     21 4 1133333333333333333333333333333333333

An entire case has been created by padding. Case will have to be deleted from dataset.

CASE NUMBER 50   CASE ID 5 9

DECKS:
  10
PADDED

130

```
JUN  7, 1984  CHECKING MERGE OF CAMPUS UNREST DATA

GOOD RECORDS:
        10 50 9 0099000000000000000000    O  O 1332232
        12 5 9SYRACUSE

***** CARDS OUT-OF-ORDER; ID DESCENDS
THIS CASE ID:  05 9
LAST CASE ID:  510

CASE NUMBER  52    CASE ID 05 9
-------------------------------
DECKS:
  12
PADDED

GOOD RECORDS:
  4910051 9112479 4144 03122112121
  1205 9                  999999  9999999

CASE NUMBER  53    CASE ID 2356
-------------------------------
  1 EXTRA CARD(S) -- NO CONSTANT
DECKS:
  10    12
PADDED

BAD RECORDS:
  123456789

CASE NUMBER  54    CASE ID 9999
-------------------------------
  1 EXTRA CARD(S) -- NO CONSTANT
DECKS:
  10    12
PADDED

BAD RECORDS:
  9999999999

NUMBER OF MISSING CARDS          8
NUMBER OF EXTRA CARDS            4
NUMBER OF DUPLICATE CARDS        3

CARDS READ              107
CASES PROCESSED          54
CASES WRITTEN            54
CASES DELETED             0
CASES WITH ERRORS         8
CARDS DELETED             7

INPUT RECORD LENGTH:     80
OUTPUT RECORD LENGTH:    80
OUTPUT BLOCK SIZE:    32720

***** Normal termination of MERCHECK $  0.12    0.09 secs
```

400
400   Deck 10 must be fixed.

The out-of-order problem is because &COPYSORT sorts using the IBM character sequence (a blank is less than zero) and &MERCHECK uses the numeric value (a blank equals zero). The out-of-order problem must be fixed before using any program that requires sorted data.

This is the other half of case 5 9. This case will be deleted from dataset. The values in
400   Deck 10 will be used to repair the 5 9 case at
400   top of page.

Case should be deleted.

Case should be deleted.

The sort problem which was uncovered does not appear in summary.

All together, 4 cases need to be deleted while 2 cases need to be repaired.

131

```
$SIGNON SDM3  PRINTER=PAGE,ONESIDED  COPIES=3 DELIVERY=ISR3 PAPER=PLAIN
Batch,Normal,Univ/Gov't
Last signon was at 14:46:15, Thu Jun 07/84
User SDM3 signed on at 09:44:39, Fri Jun 08/84

$CRE MYDICT
File "MYDICT" has been created.

$RUN ISR:OSIRIS.IV
Execution begins  09:44:51
```

C.4 Printout: Create OSIRIS Dictionary

The apostrophe in '...father s...' and
'...husband s...' has been omitted.
A single prime within primes causes
problems: the prime could have been
specified by typing it twice, e.g.
'...father ''s....

OSIRIS IV MONITOR SYSTEM
09:44:52 JUN 8, 1984
Issue &NEWS for bulletins and Usage Tax notice. Last changed 1/6/84.
&DOCR corrects directly structured datasets. SRC/CSG has writeup.

```
&DICT DICTOUT=MYDICT
DICTIONARY FOR CAMPUS UNREST DATA
NREC=2 PRINT=(DI,OUTD)
V=1  NAME='STATE                      Q1'   WID=2 COL=7 RECO=1
V=2  NAME='RESPONDENT ID              Q2'   WID=2 COL=10
V=3  NAME='NUMBER OF CALLS            Q22'  WID=1 COL=9 MD1=O
V=4  NAME='SEX                        Q23'  WID=1 COL=12 MD1=NONE
V=5  NAME='RACE                       Q24'  WID=1 MD1=O
V=6  NAME='MARITAL STATUS             Q4'   WID=1 MD1=O
V=7  NAME='AGE                        Q3'   WID=2 MD1=99
V=8  NAME='EDUCATION                  Q5'   WID=1 MD1=O TY=A
V=9  NAME='OCCUPATION                 Q7'   WID=2 MD1=O TY=C
V=10 NAME='EMPLOYMENT STATUS          Q6'   WID=1 MD1=O
V=11 NAME='FATHER S OCCUPATION        Q9'   WID=1 MD1=O COL=22
V=12 NAME='HUSBAND S OCC              Q8'   WID=2 MD1=O
V=13 NAME='CHILDREN IN COLLEGE        Q12'  WID=1 MD1=O
V=14 NAME='WORK FOR POL PARTY         Q13'  WID=1 MD1=O
V=15 NAME='STUDENT VOICE              Q14'  WID=1 MD1=O
V=16 NAME='CONSPIRACY                 Q15'  WID=1 MD1=O
V=17 NAME='BAN SDS                    Q16'  WID=1 MD1=O
V=18 NAME='VIET NAM                   Q17'  WID=1 MD1=O
V=19 NAME='LOT OF AVERAGE MAN         Q18'  WID=1 MD1=O
V=20 NAME='CHILD INTO WORLD           Q19'  WID=1 MD1=O
V=21 NAME='COUNT ON PEOPLE            Q20'  WID=1 MD1=O
V=22 NAME='LIVE FOR TODAY             Q21'  WID=1 MD1=O
V=23 NAME='NEAREST LARGE CITY         Q25'  WID=20 TY=A COL=12 RECO=2
V=24 NAME='R S COMMUNITY SIZE         Q27'  WID=1 MD1=O COL=21 RECO=1 TY=C
V=25 NAME='DIST FROM CITY             Q26'  WID=3 MD1=999 COL=32 RECO=2
V=26 NAME='TRAVEL TIME TO CITY        Q10'  WID=3 ND=1 MD1=99.9
V=27 NAME='NEW YORK TIMES             Q11'  WID=1 MD1=9 COL=40 ND=O
V=28 NAME='ANN ARBOR NEWS             Q11'  WID=1 MD1=9
V=29 NAME='DETROIT FREE PRESS         Q11'  WID=1 MD1=9
V=30 NAME='WALL STREET JOURNAL        Q11'  WID=1 MD1=9
V=31 NAME='CHRISTIAN SCIENCE MO       Q11'  WID=1 MD1=9
V=32 NAME='DAILY WORKER               Q11'  WID=1 MD1=9
V=33 NAME='WASHINGTON POST            Q11'  WID=1 MD1=9
```

133

*** DICT -- DICTIONARY CREATION AND MODIFICATION COMMAND ***

JUN 8, 1984 DICTIONARY FOR CAMPUS UNREST DATA

OUTPUT DICTIONARY

VAR#	VARIABLE NAME	GROUP	COL	WIDTH	NDEC	TYPE	MDCODE1	MDCODE2	RESP	REFNO ID
V1	STATE	Q1	0	7	2	0	C			1	1
V2	RESPONDENT ID	Q2	0	10	2	0	C			1	2
V3	NUMBER OF CALLS	Q22	0	9	1	0	C	0		1	3
V4	SEX	Q23	0	12	1	0	C			1	4
V5	RACE	Q24	0	13	1	0	C	0		1	5
V6	MARITAL STATUS	Q4	0	14	1	0	C	0		1	6
V7	AGE	Q3	0	15	2	0	C	99		1	7
V8	EDUCATION	Q5	0	17	1	0	A	0		1	8
V9	OCCUPATION	Q7	0	18	2	0	C	0		1	9
V10	EMPLOYMENT STATUS	Q6	0	20	1	0	C	0		1	10
V11	FATHER S OCCUPATION	Q9	0	22	1	0	C	0		1	11
V12	HUSBAND S OCC	Q8	0	23	2	0	C	0		1	12
V13	CHILDREN IN COLLEGE	Q12	0	25	1	0	C	0		1	13
V14	WORK FOR POL PARTY	Q13	0	26	1	0	C	0		1	14
V15	STUDENT VOICE	Q14	0	27	1	0	C	0		1	15
V16	CONSPIRACY	Q15	0	28	1	0	C	0		1	16
V17	BAN SDS	Q16	0	29	1	0	C	0		1	17
V18	VIET NAM	Q17	0	30	1	0	C	0		1	18
V19	LOT OF AVERAGE MAN	Q18	0	31	1	0	C	0		1	19
V20	CHILD INTO WORLD	Q19	0	32	1	0	C	0		1	20
V21	COUNT ON PEOPLE	Q20	0	33	1	0	C	0		1	21
V22	LIVE FOR TODAY	Q21	0	34	1	0	C	0		1	22
V23	NEAREST LARGE CITY	Q25	0	92	20	0	A	0		1	23
V24	R S COMMUNITY SIZE	Q27	0	21	1	0	C	0		1	24
V25	DIST FROM CITY	Q26	0	112	3	0	C	999		1	25
V26	TRAVEL TIME TO CITY	Q10	0	115	3	1	C	999		1	26

134

JUN 8, 1984 DICTIONARY FOR CAMPUS UNREST DATA

VAR#	VARIABLE NAME	GROUP	COL	WIDTH	NDEC	TYPE	MDCODE1	MDCODE2	RESP	REFNO	ID
V27	NEW YORK TIMES	Q11 0	120	1	0	C	9		1	27	
V28	ANN ARBOR NEWS	Q11 0	121	1	0	C	9		1	28	
V29	DETROIT FREE PRESS	Q11 0	122	1	0	C	9		1	29	
V30	WALL STREET JOURNAL	Q11 0	123	1	0	C	9		1	30	
V31	CHRISTIAN SCIENCE MO	Q11 0	124	1	0	C	9		1	31	
V32	DAILY WORKER	Q11 0	125	1	0	C	9		1	32	
V33	WASHINGTON POST	Q11 0	126	1	0	C	9		1	33	

***** Normal termination of DICT $ 0.12 $ 0.08 secs

***** The last command has been processed.
Execution terminated   09:44:53   T=0.089   RC=0 $0.22

$SIGNOFF

135

```
$SIGNON SDM3  PRINTER=PAGE,ONESIDED  COPIES=3  DELIVERY=ISR3 PAPER=PLAIN
Batch,Normal,Univ/Gov't
Last signon was at 09:44:39, Fri Jun 08/84.
User SDM3 signed on at 09:45:56, Fri Jun 08/84
```

```
$CRE NEWDICT
File "NEWDICT" has been created.
```

```
$CRE NEWDATA
File "NEWDATA" has been created.
```

```
$RUN ISR:OSIRIS.IV
Execution begins    09:46:02
```

C.5 Printout: Using &RECODE with &TRANS
to correct the amps and dashes in the
Campus Unrest dataset.

```
OSIRIS IV MONITOR SYSTEM
09:46:02 JUN  8, 1984
Issue &NEWS for bulletins and Usage Tax notice.  Last changed 1/6/84.
&DCOR corrects directly structured datasets.  SRC/CSG has writeup.

&RECODE
IF V8 EQ '0' THEN V8=0
IF V8 EQ '1' THEN V8=1
IF V8 EQ '2' THEN V8=2
IF V8 EQ '3' THEN V8=3
IF V8 EQ '4' THEN V8=4
IF V8 EQ '5' THEN V8=5
IF V8 EQ '6' THEN V8=6
IF V8 EQ '7' THEN V8=7
IF V8 EQ '8' THEN V8=8
IF V8 EQ '9' THEN V8=9
IF V8 EQ '8' THEN V8=10
IF V8 EQ '-' THEN V8=11

***** Normal termination of RECODE     $   0.08     0.11 secs


OSIRIS IV MONITOR SYSTEM
09:46:06 JUN  8, 1984

&TRANS DICTIN=MYDICT DATAIN=CUMERGED DICTOUT=NEWDICT DATAOUT=NEWDATA
RECODE AMPS AND DASHES.  REFORMAT TO ONE LOGICAL RECORD PER CASE.
R=1 V=1-33
V=8 WID=2 TYPE=C


*** TRANS - FILE TRANSFORMATIONS ***

JUN  8, 1984  RECODE AMPS AND DASHES.   REFORMAT TO ONE LOGICAL RECORD PER CASE.          TRANS     1

THE OUTPUT DICTIONARY WILL BE TYPE 5

ILLEGAL CHARACTERS IN THE DATA WILL
BE TREATED AS MISSING DATA 1

33 VARIABLES AND    54 CASES WRITTEN; LRECL =   62    BLKSIZE = 32736

***** Normal termination of TRANS     $   0.11     0.12 secs

***** The last command has been processed
Execution terminated   09:46:07  T=0.245   RC=0   $0.31


$SIGNOFF
```

The logical record length is now 62 characters.

137

```
$SIGNON SDM3  PRINTER=PAGE,ONESIDED  COPIES=3 DELIVERY=ISR3 PAPER=PLAIN
Batch,Normal,Univ/Gov't
Last signon was at 09:45:56, Fri Jun 08/84
User SDM3 signed on at 09:47:05, Fri Jun 08/84


$RUN ISR:OSIRIS.IV
Execution begins  09:47:09



OSIRIS IV MONITOR SYSTEM
09:47:09 JUN  8, 1984
Issue &NEWS for bulletins and Usage Tax notice. Last changed 1/6/84.
&DCOR corrects directly structured datasets.  SRC/CSG has writeup.

&WCC DICTIN=NEWDICT DATAIN=NEWDATA
CHECK WILD CODES
ID=(1,2,23)
V=3,5,6,18 CODES=0-3
V=4 CODES=1-2
V=12 MIN=O MAX=14
V=17 CODES=0-2
V=1-2,7-11,13-16,19-33
```

The WCC program rounds non-integer data before checking. The decimal place in V26, Travel Time To City, has been rounded.

Note that ' ' and '0 '(a full field of blanks and embedded blanks) are considered bad data. Remember that &WCC has not changed the data. A printout is the only output from the program.

```
*** WCC -- WILD CODE CHECKER ***

JUN  8, 1984  CHECK WILD CODES

***** WARNING: 1 OR MORE VARIABLES ROUNDED

ID=O1 O7 DETROIT
      V4  SEX               Q23 WILD CODE:  4
      V12 HUSBAND S OCC      Q8  WILD CODE: 23

ID=O2 O1 MESA
      V12 HUSBAND S OCC      Q8 BAD DATA VALUE: 'BB'

ID=O2 1O PHOENIX
      V11 FATHER S OCCUPATION  Q9 BAD DATA VALUE: 'I'

ID=O4 O7 GREENSBORO
      V5  RACE              Q24 WILD CODE:  9
      V6  MARITAL STATUS     Q4  WILD CODE:  9

ID=O4 11  V4  SEX           Q23 BAD DATA VALUE: ' '

ID=O5 O4 ROCHESTER
      V18 VIET NAM           Q17 WILD CODE:  4
      V17 BAN SDS            Q16 WILD CODE:  3

ID=O5 O9 SYRACUSE
      V4  SEX               Q23 BAD DATA VALUE: ' '
      V25 DIST FROM CITY     Q26 BAD DATA VALUE: ' '
      V26 TRAVEL TIME TO CITY  Q10 BAD DATA VALUE: 'O'

ID=23 56  V4  SEX           Q23 BAD DATA VALUE: ' '

ID=99 99  V4  SEX           Q23 BAD DATA VALUE: ' '

      54 ENTRIES CHECKED FOR   33 VARIABLES
      14 WILD CODES
       9 ENTRIES WITH WILD CODES

***** Normal termination of WCC    $ 0.09    0.10 secs

***** The last command has been processed.
Execution terminated  09:47:10  T=0.109  RC=0  $0.19


$SIGNOFF
```

139

```
$SIGNON SDM3  PRINTER=PAGE,ONESIDED  COPIES=3 DELIVERY=ISR3 PAPER=PLAIN
Batch,Normal,Univ/Gov't
Last signon was at 09:47:05, Fri Jun 08/84
User SDM3 signed on at 09:48:09, Fri Jun 08/84


$CREATE DI4
File "DI4" has been created.

$CREATE DA4
File "DA4" has been created.

$RUN ISR:OSIRIS.IV
Execution begins   09:48:15




OSIRIS IV MONITOR SYSTEM
09:48:15 JUN  8, 1984
  Issue &NEWS for bulletins and Usage Tax notice. Last changed 1/6/84.
8DCOR corrects directly structured datasets.  SRC/CSG has writeup.

&FCOR DICTIN=NEWDICT DATAIN=NEWDATA DICTOUT=DI4 DATAOUT=DA4
  EXCLUDE V1=5 AND V2=9 AND V7=47
  RUN TO MAKE CORRECTIONS ON CAMPUS UNREST DATA
  ID=1,2 PRINT=(DEL,CORR,DI)
```

```
***FCOR---FILE CORRECTIONS ***

JUN  8, 1984   RUN TO MAKE CORRECTIONS ON CAMPUS UNREST DATA

INPUT DATA FILE IS RECTANGULAR

INPUT DICTIONARY RECORDS WILL BE PRINTED

CORRECTED RECORDS WILL BE PRINTED

DELETED RECORDS WILL BE PRINTED

A KEYWORD ERROR WILL CAUSE
THE INSTRUCTION RECORD TO BE SKIPPED

AN OUT OF ORDER INSTRUCTION RECORD WILL CAUSE
THE INSTRUCTION RECORD TO BE SKIPPED

A DUPLICATE INSTRUCTION RECORD WILL CAUSE
THE INSTRUCTION RECORD TO BE SKIPPED

A DUPLICATE DATA RECORD WILL CAUSE
THE INSTRUCTION TO BE CARRIED OUT AND PROCESSING TO CONTINUE
```

141

Two complete pages are omitted here;
FCOR 2 and FCOR 3 were the printout of
the dictionary.

```
JUN  8, 1984   RUN TO MAKE CORRECTIONS ON CAMPUS UNREST DATA
ID=(1,7) V4=1,V12=O

...THE FOLLOWING RECORD HAS BEEN CORRECTED:
 1 7111372021227001222110211DETROIT          5  O  0221232
ID=(2.1) V12=O

...THE FOLLOWING RECORD HAS BEEN CORRECTED:
 2 1211124061227001132112121MESA             3  O  01332313
ID=(2.1O) V11=1

...THE FOLLOWING RECORD HAS BEEN CORRECTED:
 210121248101 111 0411121112PHOENIX          9 50 153333233
ID=(3.5) V23=FRESNO,V25=OOO,V26=OOO,V27=3,V28=9,V30=3,V31=3,V32=3,V33=3

...THE FOLLOWING RECORD HAS BEEN CORRECTED:
 3 5111260111 113 0322212122FRESNO            1OOOOOO3923333
ID=(4.7) V5=1 V6=O

...THE FOLLOWING RECORD HAS BEEN CORRECTED:
 ..712105205132112111211102GREENSBORO         9 81 221333331
ID=(4.11) DEL

...THE FOLLOWING RECORD HAS BEEN DELETED:
 411O 0099OOOOOOOOOOOOOOOOOO                   0999999999999
ID=(5.4) V18=3,V17=2

...THE FOLLOWING RECORD HAS BEEN CORRECTED:
 5 41123290681601113231121ROCHESTER          7 56 121331333
ID=(5.9) V3=1,V4=1,V5=1,V62,V7=47,V8=9 V1O=1,V11=4,V12=O,V13=3,V14=1,V15=2,V16=2,V17=1,V18=1,V19=2,V20=1,V21=2,V22=1,V24=4,V25=999,
V26=99.9

...THE FOLLOWING RECORD HAS BEEN CORRECTED:
 5 911124709001400312211212ISYRACUSE          4999991332232
ID=(23.56) DEL

...THE FOLLOWING RECORD HAS BEEN DELETED:
 23560 0099OOOOOOOOOOOOOOOOOO                  0999999999999
ID=(99.99) DEL

...THE FOLLOWING RECORD HAS BEEN DELETED:
 99990 0099OOOOOOOOOOOOOOOOOO                  0999999999999

   5O RECORDS WERE PROCESSED WITH LRECL   62 AND BLOCKSIZE 32736

***** Normal termination of FCOR     $   0.22    0.16 secs

***** The last command has been processed.
Execution terminated   09:48:18  T=0.169  RC=O  $O.32


$SIGNOFF
```

```
$SIGNON SDM3  PRINTER=PAGE,ONESIDED  COPIES=3 DELIVERY=ISR3 PAPER=PLAIN
Batch,Normal,Univ/Gov't
Last signon was at 09:48:09, Fri Jun 08/84
User SDM3 signed on at 09:49:15, Fri Jun 08/84


$RUN ISR:OSIRIS.IV
Execution begins    09:49:20



OSIRIS IV MONITOR SYSTEM
09:49:21 JUN  8, 1984
Issue $NEWS for bulletins and Usage Tax notice. Last changed 1/6/84.
&DCOR corrects directly structured datasets.   SRC/CSG has writeup.

&RECODE
    MDATA R16(O),R17(O)
    R16=BRAC(V16,3=1,2=2,1=3,ELSE=O)
    R17=BRAC(V17,2=1,1=3,ELSE=O)
    MDATA R100(O)
    R100=O
    R101=O
    IF NOT MDATA(V15) THEN R101=R101+1 AND R100=R100+V15
    IF NOT MDATA(R16) THEN R101=R101+1 AND R100=R100+R16
    IF NOT MDATA(R17) THEN R101=R101+1 AND R100=R100+R17
    IF NOT MDATA(V18) THEN R101=R101+1 AND R100=R100+V18
    IF R101 LT 2 THEN R100=O ELSE R100=R100/R101
    NAME R100 'CONSERVATIVE INDEX'

***** Normal termination of RECODE  $   0.07    0.11 secs



OSIRIS IV MONITOR SYSTEM
09:49:23 JUN  8, 1984

&DSLIST DICTIN=DI4 DATAIN=DA4
CHECK THE INDEX
R=1 V=15-18,R16-R17,R100-R101 P=DI C=(1,50,5) SEQ
```

143

```
*** DSLIST -- DATASET LISTING COMMAND ***

JUN  8, 1984   CHECK THE INDEX
```

VAR#	VARIABLE NAME	GROUP	COL	WIDTH	NDEC	TYPE	MDCODE1	MDCODE2	RESP	REFNO	ID
R101	VARIABLE R101	0	0	4	2	F			1	0	
R100	CONSERVATIVE INDEX	0	0	4	2	F	0		1	0	
R17	VARIABLE R17	0	0	4	2	F	0		1	0	
R16	VARIABLE R16	0	0	4	2	F	0		1	0	
V15	STUDENT VOICE	Q14	0	21	1	C	0		1	15	
V16	CONSPIRACY	Q15	0	22	1	C	0		1	16	
V17	BAN SDS	Q16	0	23	1	C	0		1	17	
V18	VIET NAM	Q17	0	24	1	C	0		1	18	

```
JUN  8, 1984   CHECK THE INDEX
```

SEQ	V15	V16	V17	V18	R16	R17	R100	R101
5	1	1	1	2	2.00	3.00	2.00	4.00
10	1	0	2	2	2.00	3.00	1.67	3.00
15	1	2	1	2	2.00	1.00	1.67	3.00
20	1	2	2	2	2.00	3.00	2.00	4.00
25	2	2	1	1	2.00	3.00	2.25	4.00
30	2	3	2	2	1.00	1.00	1.50	4.00
35	2	1	1	1	1.00	1.00	1.50	4.00
40	1	1	2	1	3.00	3.00	2.00	4.00
45	2	2	2	1	2.00	1.00	1.50	4.00
50	2	3	2	1	1.00	1.00	1.00	4.00

```
50 CASES READ
10 CASES PRINTED

***** Normal termination of DSLIST  $  0.10   0.07 secs
```

Appendix D

A HYPOTHETICAL HIERARCHICAL DATASET

Figures D.1 to D.3 below are listings (using the OSIRIS &DSLIST command) of three hypothical standard rectangular OSIRIS datasets, one for states, one for cities, and one for respondents. These three datasets form a hierarchy as described in section 8.4. Figure D.4 is the printout of the &SBUILD run (see section 8.5) that created a structured dataset from these data. The four datasets are publicly available on University of Michigan account (CCID) SDM3. They may be read or copied from that CCID. The file names are DISTA, DASTA, DICIT, DACIT, DIRES, DARES, DISTRUCT and DASTRUCT.

JUN 14, 1984   EXAMPLE--FAKE STATE DATA

VAR#	VARIABLE NAME	GROUP	COL	WIDTH	NDEC	TYPE	MDCODE1	MDCODE2	RESP	REFNO	ID
V1	STATE ID	0	1	1	0	C			1	1	1
V2	REGION	0	2	1	0	C			1	2	2
V3	STATE SIZE	0	3	1	0	C			1	3	3

JUN 14, 1984   EXAMPLE--FAKE STATE DATA

V1	V2	V3
1	1	2
2	2	2
3	1	4
4	3	3
5	1	1
6	2	1
7	2	2
8	2	3

LAST CASE IN FILE PRINTED ABOVE

8 CASES READ
8 CASES PRINTED

***** Normal termination of DSLIST $ 0.07   0.10 secs

D.1   Dictionary and Data for States dataset.

[1]In this and some of the following printouts, material that originally appeared on two or more pages has been consolidated by cut and paste.

146

JUN 14, 1984   EXAMPLE--FAKE CITY DATA

DSLIST   1

VAR#	VARIABLE NAME	GROUP	COL	WIDTH	NDEC	TYPE	MDCODE1	MDCODE2	RESP	REFNO	ID
V1	STATE ID	0	1	1	0	C			1	1	
V2	CITY ID	0	2	2	0	C			1	2	
V3	TYPE OF CITY GOV	0	4	1	0	C			1	3	
V4	CITY SIZE	0	5	1	0	C			1	4	

JUN 14, 1984   EXAMPLE--FAKE CITY DATA

DSLIST   2

V1	V2	V3	V4
4	1	3	1
6	2	1	3
2	3	1	1
1	4	2	2
3	5	1	1
8	6	1	1
2	7	3	1
1	8	2	1
7	9	1	2
7	10	2	2
7	11	2	1
8	12	3	1
4	13	1	2
4	14	1	1
3	15	2	1
2	16	1	2
1	17	2	3
2	18	1	3
8	19	3	3
7	20	2	3

LAST CASE IN FILE PRINTED ABOVE

20 CASES READ
20 CASES PRINTED

***** Normal termination of DSLIST $ 0.04   0.06 secs

D.2   Dictionary and Data for Cities dataset.

147

*** DSLIST -- DATASET LISTING COMMAND ***

JUN 14, 1984   EXAMPLE--FAKE PERSON DATA

VAR#	VARIABLE NAME	GROUP	COL	WIDTH	NDEC	TYPE	MDCODE1	MDCODE2	RESP	REFNO	ID
V1	STATE ID	0	1	1	0	C			1	1	1
V2	CITY ID	0	2	2	0	C			1	2	2
V3	RESP ID	0	4	2	0	C			1	3	3
V4	SAT WITH STATE GOV	0	6	1	0	C			1	4	4
V5	SAT WITH CITY GOV	0	7	1	0	C			1	5	5
V6	SAT WITH TRANSPORTATION	0	8	1	0	C			1	6	6

JUN 14, 1984   EXAMPLE--FAKE PERSON DATA

V1	V2	V3	V4	V5	V6
8	6	1	3	1	2
2	7	2	2	2	1
8	6	3	1	3	1
3	5	4	4	3	1
8	19	5	3	2	1
8	19	6	3	1	3
7	20	7	4	3	3
3	15	8	2	2	1
2	7	9	2	1	3
3	5	10	2	3	1
1	8	11	1	1	2
8	6	12	2	3	1
4	14	13	2	1	1
2	16	14	3	1	2
7	11	15	3	1	1
2	9	16	4	1	2
2	8	17	2	3	3
1	8	18	1	1	3
7	9	19	1	1	3
4	1	20	4	2	1
6	2	21	4	2	3
2	3	22	3	3	1
1	4	23	2	1	1
1	4	24	1	1	1
2	3	25	1	1	1
2	3	26	1	1	1
7	10	27	2	1	1
8	12	28	1	1	1
4	13	29	3	1	1

V1	V2	V3	V4	V5	V6
4	14	30	2	2	1
2	18	31	1	2	1
2	19	32	4	1	1
8	16	33	3	3	3
3	12	34	3	1	3
2	5	35	1	1	2
7	7	36	3	3	3
7	9	37	4	1	1
2	11	38	4	3	3
7	11	39	4	1	1
2	16	40	2	1	2
8	12	41	2	3	3
7	5	42	2	1	1
3	9	43	4	3	3
5	11	44	4	1	2
3	8	45	1	1	2
1	8	46	3	3	2
7	9	47	3	2	2
7	11	48	3	2	2
7	11	49	2	1	3
2	16	50	3	3	1

LAST CASE IN FILE PRINTED ABOVE

50 CASES READ
50 CASES PRINTED

D.3 Dictionary and Data for Respondents dataset.

```
16:45:23 JUN 14. 1984
Issue &NEWS for bulletins and Usage Tax notice.  Last changed 1/6/84.
&DCOR corrects directly structured datasets.  SRC/CSG has writeup.

&SBUILD DICTIN1=DISTA DICTIN2=DICIT DICTIN3=DIRES DICTOUT=DISTRUCT DATAIN1=DASTA DATAIN2=DACIT DATAIN3=DARES DATAOUT=DASTRUCT DATATE
MP=-Z
MY STRUCTURED FILE
PR=OUTDICT
GNUM=1 LEVEL=1 V=ALL NAME='STATE GROUP' INFI=IN1
GNUM=2 LEVEL=2 V=ALL RENU=V1O1 NAME='CITY GROUP' INFI=IN2 LINK=(G2.V1:G1.V1)
GNUM=3 LEVEL=3 V=ALL RENU=V2O1 NAME='RESP GROUP' INFI=IN3 ID=3 LINK=(G3.V1:G1.V1,G3.V2:G2.V2)
```

D.4 Printout from &SBUILD run to create structured
dataset of States, Cities and Respondents.

```
*** SBUILD - STRUCTURED FILE BUILDING COMMAND ***

JUN 14, 1984  MY STRUCTURED FILE

SORTING SCHEMA (GROUP IDENTIFICATION VARIABLES AND CONSTANTS):

GROUP LEVO1 LEVO2 LEVO3
      VAR   VAR   VAR
001   V1    V2
002   V1    V2    V3
003   V1    V2    V3

*** THE NUMBER OF VARIABLES IN GROUP 1   IS 3

*** THE NUMBER OF RECORDS IN GROUP  1    IS 8

*** THE NUMBER OF VARIABLES IN GROUP 2   IS 4

*** THE NUMBER OF RECORDS IN GROUP  2    IS 20

*** THE NUMBER OF VARIABLES IN GROUP 3   IS 6

*** THE NUMBER OF RECORDS IN GROUP  3    IS 50
```

150

*** OUTPUT DICTIONARY:

VAR#	VARIABLE NAME	GROUP	COL	WIDTH	NDEC	TYPE	MDCODE1	MDCODE2	RESP	REFNO	ID
V1	STATE ID	1	9	1	0	C			1	1	1
V2	REGION	1	10	1	0	C			1	2	
V3	STATE SIZE	1	11	1	0	C			1	3	
V101	STATE ID	2	9	1	0	C			1	1	
V102	CITY ID	2	10	2	0	C			1	2	
V103	TYPE OF CITY GOV	2	12	1	0	C			1	3	
V104	CITY SIZE	2	13	1	0	C			1	4	
V201	STATE ID	3	9	1	0	C			1	1	
V202	CITY ID	3	10	2	0	C			1	2	
V203	RESP ID	3	12	2	0	C			1	3	
V204	SAT WITH STATE GOV	3	14	1	0	C			1	4	
V205	SAT WITH CITY GOV	3	15	1	0	C			1	5	
V206	SAT WITH TRANSPORTATION	3	16	1	0	C			1	6	

THE STRUCTURED DATA WILL HAVE:

    LRECL= 20
    BLKSIZE= 32764
    RECFM=VBS

THE SORT FIELD BEGINS IN POSITION 8
FOR A LENGTH OF 5

ALL VALUES INCLUDE THE FOUR-POSITION RECORD LENGTH FIELD BEFORE EACH DATA RECORD

*** NUMBER OF OUTPUT RECORDS: 78

***** Normal termination of SBUILD $ 0.28   0.33 secs

***** The last command has been processed.

151

SYSTEM FLOWCHART FOR PROCESSING CAMPUS UNREST DATA

Step   Filename

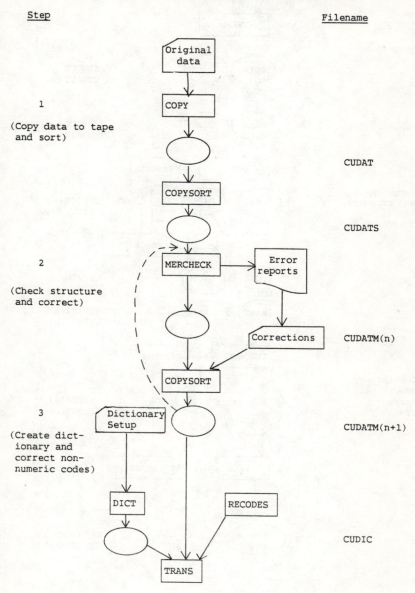

1

(Copy data to tape
and sort)

2

(Check structure
and correct)

3

(Create dict-
ionary and
correct non-
numeric codes)

System Flowchart (cont.)

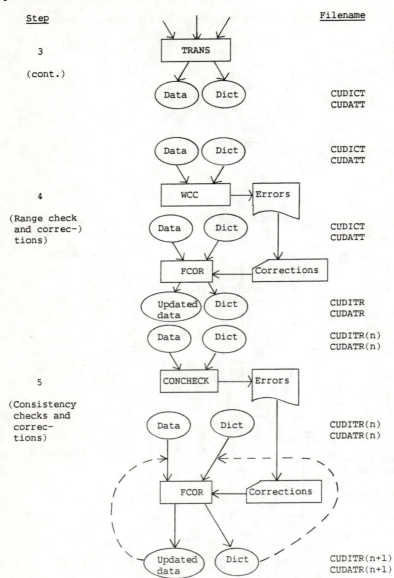

3

(cont.)

CUDICT
CUDATT

CUDICT
CUDATT

4

(Range check
and correc-)
tions)

CUDICT
CUDATT

CUDITR
CUDATR

CUDITR(n)
CUDATR(n)

5

(Consistency
checks and
correc-
tions)

CUDITR(n)
CUDATR(n)

CUDITR(n+1)
CUDATR(n+1)

Computer Run Record

Project   Campus Unrest Survey

Run id	Step	Pass	Program	Input	Output	Description	Outcome	Date
JO1269	1		COPY		CUDAT		V	6/3/81
JO1372	1		COPYSORT	CUDAT	CUDATS	sort data	V	6/4/81
JO1391	2	1	MERCHECK	CUDATS	CUDATM1		failed	6/5/81
JO1425	2	1	MERCHECK	CUDATS	CUDATM1		V	6/7/81
JO1564	2	1	COPYSORT	CUDATM1	CUDATM2		V	6/9/81
JO1653	2	2	MERCHECK	CUDATM2	--		V	6/10/81
JO1772	2	1	TRANS	CUDATM2	CUDATT		V	6/13/81
JO1946	3	1	WCC	CUDATT			V	6/14/81
JO2024	3	1	FCOR	CUDATMT	CUDATR1		V	6/19/81
JO2025	3	2	WCC	CUDATR1			V	6/19/81
JO2214	3	2	FCOR	CUDATR1	CUDATR2		V	6/25/81

etc.

Tape Record

Tape   C1962

File	Dataset Name	LRECL	BLKSIZE	N	Job created	Comment	Date Created
1	CUDAT	80	4000	615	JO1269	Original data	6/3/81
2	CUDATM1	80	4000	630	JO1425	Data with some MERCHECK errors corrected	6/7/81
3	CUDICT	80	1600	90	JO1846		6/13/81
4	CUDATT	80	4000	630	JO1772		6/13/81
5	CUDATR2	314	3140	96	JO2025		6/19/81

etc.

Appendix F

EXAMPLES OF ERRORS

Chapter 1, section 1.12, classified types of errors as either syntatical or logical in either job control language or program control language. When trying to figure out why a job has failed it helps to be aware of these various types of errors.

Figure F.1 shows examples of errors. The error in the upper left corner of the first page is an MTS error. This error is fairly evident, at least after a bit of staring. For more complicated MTS errors, MTS Manual [9] is the reference to consult. The MTS error in the lower left corner of the first page (selected to match the OS error to its right) is an MTS logical error which was detected by the OSIRIS monitor (see the final paragraph of section 1.7). The errors shown under the column heading OS can occur when using an IBM 360 or 370 running under the OS operating system. These errors are discussed in IBM System/360 and System/370 Operating System Messages and Codes [6]. The second page of the figure shows examples of OSIRIS errors; the OSIRIS IV Manual [10] is the reference to consult for help with these errors. Note, however, that the manual won't help much with the logical error at the bottom of the page.

Job Control Language

Syntax Errors

MTS

```
$SIGNON SDM3
DAISY
$RUN ISR:OSRIS.IV

"ISR:OSRIS.IV" DOES NOT EXIST
```

OS

```
//MOO7541 JOB (,
//  468363,S62.,2),RATTENBURY,CLASS=B
//  EXEC OSRIS
IEF612I  PROCEDURE NOT FOUND
```

OSIRIS is misspelled

Logical Errors

MTS

```
$MOUNT C3116A 9TP *T* VOL=77B1
C3116A 9TP *T* VOL=77B1
*T* (C3116A): Mounted on T210
$RUN ISR:OSRIS.IV
&DSLIST DICTIN=*T*(DSN=DICTABC,FI=1) -
DATAIN=*T*(DSN=DATAABC,FI=2)
EXAMPLE OF ERROR
V=1-10

****DICTIN FILE NAME CONFLICT

***** ABNORMAL TERMINATION OF DSLIST
```

OS

```
//  EXEC COPY
//DATAIN DD DSN=ABC,VOL=SER=SCR1,UNIT=TAPE
IEF236I ALLOC. FOR MOO7317 GO
IEF237I OE3 ALLOCATED TO SYSPRINT
IEF237I 282 ALLOCATED TO SYSUT1
IEC139I 813-04,MOO7317,GO,SYSUT1,282.SCR1      .ABC
COMPLETION CODE - SYSTEM=813 USER=OOOO
IEF285I    ABC                                         DELETED
IEF285I    VOL SER NOS= SCR1
```

System abnormal termination (abend) produced by IBM OS operating system. The
completion code appears after the alloca-
tion messages. A 813 means that the DSNAME
specified for an input tape dataset on
the DD card does not match the name in
the header label for that dataset.

Program Control Language

OSIRIS

Syntax error

```
8DSLIST DICTIN=DI  DATAIN=DA
EXAMPLE OF SYNTAX ERROR
V1-V1O

***** SYNTAX ERROR: V1-V
***** "V1O " MUST BE FOLLOWED BY "="

SHOULD BE V=1-10
```

Logical error

The program control cards were:

```
8DSLIST DICTIN=DI  DATAIN=DA
INCLUDE V1=1 AND V1=2
LOGICAL ERROR
V=1-10
```

The program executed. The last three lines of the printout were:

```
O CASES READ
O CASES PRINTED

***** Normal termination of DSLIST
```

Fatal filter. It's impossible for a case to have both a 1 and a 2 on V1.

Fig. F.1. Examples of Errors (continued)

159

Appendix G

RUNNING OSIRIS FROM A TERMINAL AT THE UNIVERSITY OF MICHIGAN

The current version of OSIRIS was designed to be easy to run from a terminal. There are several ways of doing this. One way is shown in the example terminal session reproduced in Fig. G.1. In this example the MTS
command $EDIT (abbreviated ED or $ED) is used to enter the OSIRIS command
and its associated control cards into a temporary file. OSIRIS is then run
with the assignment SCARDS= the file where the setup was stored. In the
example the printout from &ANOVA was printed at the terminal as the program
was running. Alternatively, the $RUN command might have been.

        $RUN ISR:OSIRIS.IV SCARDS=-SETUP SPRINT=-PO

in which case the printout would have been put in the temporary file -PO.
After the message ***** NO MORE RUN COMMANDS appears on the terminal printout the user can copy the printout to the terminal using the command.

        $COPY -PO

or he can copy the last 20 lines

        $COPY -PO(LAST-20)

or he can copy the printout to *PRINT*. Copying a file to *PRINT* means it
is printed by a line or page printer at the Computing Center (or NUBS or
UNYN if you give a special setting). A receipt number is printed at the
terminal; the user takes the receipt number to the Computing Center Output
Window to claim his output. For a printout of many pages it is handy to
put the printout in a file, copy the last few lines to the terminal to
check that the run seems to be OK, and then to route the full printout to
PRINT. A command to copy to *PRINT* might be.

        $COPY -PO *PRINT*

A slight variation on the example in Fig. G.1 is to prestore only the
control cards for a command, but not the command itself. If this is done,
the user would, in our example, prestore three control cards and then

        $RUN ISR:OSIRIS.IV
        &ANOVA SOURCE=-SETUP

The SOURCE= assignment can be used to designate control cards for any
OSIRIS command.

For most commands prestoring control cards is a matter of taste; as we
shall see below it is also possible to run OSIRIS in an interactive mode.
However, prestoring (probably in a permanent file) is highly recommended
for long recodes (which might be reused or which might have errors not
detected until the end of the recode). It is also useful for &DICT (it is
not unusual to have hundreds of Variable Descriptor Statements - and to
have an error in the first run). The SOURCE= assignment is also used with
&MATRIX to make a matrix, generated say by &MDC, available to analysis
program on a later run. Commands such as

        &RECODE   SOURCE=CUNEWVARS

161

or

&DICT   SOURCE=MAKEDICT

or

&MATRIX   SOURCE=MYMAT

where CUNEWVARS, MAKEDICT and MYMAT contain all the control cards for the
command are very useful.

OSIRIS can also be run in an interactive mode. An example terminal session in the interactive mode is shown in Fig. G.2. Working in the prompt-
and-answer mode rather than a pre-storing mode has the advantage that most
simple syntactical errors will be spotted by the command and the user can
type the correction immediately. Most users like to use a combination of
pre-storing (for recodes especially) and interaction (for simple commands).
For example, the user might use $EDIT to prestore a set of recode state-
ments to create indices and then, interactively (waiting for response!),
type the following series of lines:

```
$RUN ISR:OSIRIS.IV
&RECODE SOURCE=INDEXCREATE          Makes the recode stmts.
&REGRESSION DICTING=DI1 DATAIN=DA1  available to the command
USING INDICES AS PREDICTORS
R=1 PRNT=DICT                       Calls on the recode stmts.
DEPV=20 V=R1-R6
&END
```

```
%Merit:Hermes (ISR12C:HW01:AJ832:EDIT=MTS)

Which Host?um
    MTS Ann Arbor (AB18-00529)

#   Users, please  $COPY *NIGHTS

#NUBS WILL BE DOWN UNTIL FURTHER NOTICE
#$signon sdm3
#Enter password.
?
#Terminal,Normal,Univ/Gov't
#Last signon was at 10:53:14, Tue Jun 12/84
#User SDM3 signed on at 12:54:49, Tue Jun 12/84
#ed -setup
:i
?&anova dictin=di4 datain=da4
?this setup is prestored
?*
?v=4 depv=22
?
:p /f
:   1       &anova dictin=di4 datain=da4
:   2       this setup is prestored
:   3       *
:   4       v=4 depv=22
:st
#$run isr:osiris.iv scards=-setup
```

MTS SIGNON PROCEDURE

MTS $ED COMMAND WILL BE USED TO PUT LINES IN FILE -SETUP
FAST INSERTION MODE OF $ED COMMAND IS INVOKED

FOUR LINES ARE STORED IN FILE. -SETUP

BLANK LINE SIGNALS END OF FAST INSERTION MODE
COMMAND TO $ED TO PRINT THE FILE

FILE IS PRINTED

STOP THE EDITOR
RUN OSIRIS. SCARDS IS SET EQUAL TO FILE
CONTAINING THE SETUP

THE OUTPUT FROM THE ANOVA COMMAND IS
PRINTED AT THE TERMINAL.

```
OSIRIS IV MONITOR SYSTEM
12:57:06 JUN 12, 1984
> Issue &NEWS for bulletins and Usage Tax notice.  Last changed 1/6/84.
> &DCOR corrects directly structured datasets.  SRC/CSG has writeup.

&ANOVA DICTIN=DI4 DATAIN=DA4
THIS SETUP IS PRESTORED
*
V=4 DEPV=22
```

163

```
*** ANOVA -- ONE WAY ANALYSIS OF VARIANCE ***

JUN 12, 1984  THIS SETUP IS PRESTORED

THE FOLLOWING TABLES WERE REQUESTED:

TABLE #  CONTROL VAR.  DEPEND. VAR.

   1      V4            V22

50 CASES PASSED THE FILTER

TABLE 1

CONTROL VARIABLE = V4      SEX             Q23
DEPEND. VARIABLE = V22     LIVE FOR TODAY  Q21

  CODES    N     WEIGHT-SUM    %      MEAN    S.D.(ESTIM.)   SUM OF X        %      SUM OF X-SQUARE   CODE NAME
   1      27      27.00      58.7    1.519       0.509       .4100000E+02   56.2     .6900000E+02
   2      19      19.00      41.3    1.684       0.478       .3200000E+02   43.8     .5800000E+02

  TOT     46      46.00     100.0    1.587       0.498       .7300000E+02  100.0     .1270000E+03


   TOTAL SUM OF SQUARES          =   .1115217E+02
   FOR  2 GROUPS ,          ETA  =   .1656920E+00
   FOR  2 GROUPS ,        ETASQ  =   .274538 4E-01
   FOR  2 GROUPS , ETA(ADJ)      =   .7314725E-01
   FOR  2 GROUPS , ETASQ(ADJ)    =   .5350520E-02
   BETWEEN MEANS SUM OF SQUARES  =   .3061700E+00
   WITHIN GROUPS SUM OF SQUARES  =   .1084600E+02
   F( 1, 44)                     =   1.242
   PROBABILITY(F)                =   0.27


***** Normal termination of ANOVA      $  0.06    0.09 secs


OSIRIS IV MONITOR SYSTEM
12:57:21 JUN 12, 1984

***** The last command has been processed. 'Bye.
#
```

Example of running OSIRIS from a terminal at
The University of Michigan. In this example the
&ANOVA command and its associated control
cards are prestored in a temporary disk
file called -SETUP.

Fig. G.1

```
$run lsr:osiris.iv

OSIRIS IV MONITOR SYSTEM
12:58:13 JUN 12, 1984
> Issue &NEWS for bulletins and Usage Tax notice. Last changed 1/6/84.
> &DCOR corrects directly structured datasets. SRC/CSG has writeup.

&COMMAND?
?&comment: now I'll do the same thing in interactive mode
?&anova dictin=di4 datain=da4

ENTER A LABEL TO TITLE EACH PAGE OR A FILTER STATEMENT:
?this setup is being entered interactively

ENTER PARAMETER STATEMENT:
?*

ENTER PROBLEM STATEMENT:
?v=4 depv=22
?&end
```

EXAMPLE OF USING THE COMMAND &COMMENT--HAS NO EFFECT ON THE RUN
THE &ANOVA COMMAND

THE PROGRAM PROMPTS
   MY ANSWER

PROGRAM
   MY ANSWER (ALL THE DEFAULTS)

PROGRAM
   MY ANSWER
   MY SIGNAL THAT THERE ARE NO FURTHER PROBLEM STATEMENTS

THE OUTPUT FROM THE &ANOVA COMMAND IS PRINTED AT THE TERMINAL

```
*** ANOVA -- ONE WAY ANALYSIS OF VARIANCE ***                    ANOVA    1

JUN 12, 1984   THIS SETUP IS BEING ENTERED INTERACTIVELY

THE FOLLOWING TABLES WERE REQUESTED:

TABLE #    CONTROL VAR.    DEPEND. VAR.
   1         V4              V22
```

50 CASES PASSED THE FILTER

TABLE 1

CONTROL VARIABLE = V4   SEX   Q23
DEPEND. VARIABLE = V22   LIVE FOR TODAY   Q21

CODES	N	WEIGHT-SUM	%	MEAN	S.D.(ESTIM.)	SUM OF X	%	SUM OF X-SQUARE	CODE NAME
1	27	27.00	58.7	1.519	0.509	.4100000E+02	56.2	.6900000E+02	
2	19	19.00	41.3	1.684	0.478	.3200000E+02	43.8	.5800000E+02	
TOT	46	46.00	100.0	1.587	0.498	.7300000E+02	100.0	.1270000E+03	

```
TOTAL SUM OF SQUARES          =  .1115217E+02
FOR  2 GROUPS ,         ETA   =  .1656920E+00
FOR  2 GROUPS ,       ETASQ   =  .2745384E-01
FOR  2 GROUPS ,    ETA(ADJ)   =  .7314725E-01
FOR  2 GROUPS ,  ETASQ(ADJ)   =  .5330520E-02
BETWEEN MEANS SUM OF SQUARES  =  .3061700E+00
WITHIN GROUPS SUM OF SQUARES  =  .1084600E+02
F( 1,  44)                    =  1.242
PROBABILITY(F)                =  0.27

***** Normal termination of ANOVA    $  0.06    $  0.07 secs
```

```
&COMMAND?
?&end

&COMMAND?
?&mts
#$signoff
#SDM3 12:54:49 to 13:00:36, Tue Jun 12/84
#Terminal,Normal,Univ/Gov't
#Elapsed time       5.766 minutes
#CPU time used       .531 seconds      $.14
#CPU storage VMI     .366 page-min.    $.29
#Wait storage VMI   3.25 page-hr.      $.03
#Page-ins            210
#Disk I/O            646
#   Approximate cost of this run:      $.45

#Disk storage charge  467 page-hr.     $.03
#   Approximate remaining balance:  $103.70
#   Indirect cost surcharge:         $.08
#The 17% indirect cost surcharge has not been deducted from
#your MTS account, but will be applied to your monthly bill.

2H01:ISR12C-ABD1:UM18 Connection closed
```

Fig. C.2

Example of running OSIRIS from a terminal at The University of M.chigan. In this example the command and the associated control cards are entered interactively in response to prompts.

166

Appendix H

RUNNING OSIRIS IV UNDER THE IBM 360/370 OPERATING SYSTEM

In Chapter 1, the control program Michigan Terminal System, MTS, was introduced. In this Appendix a widely used control program, the IBM Operating System, OS, which runs on IBM's 360/370 series of computers will be described briefly.

It will be recalled from Chapter 1 that there are three basic types of information that the control program needs from the user: an account number; the name of the required applications program; and information about the input and output files required. The control language for giving instructions to OS is called Job Control Language (JCL).

Job Control Language statements are prepared by the user in a special language and punched onto cards or entered from a terminal. There are three types of statements.

(i)   Job statements for signaling the start of a new job and specifying the user's account number, and such things as estimates of computer time required, amount of printed output, etc.

e.g.,   //J1234567   (499999,TAB,,2,,,2), WILSON
         JOB name   *Accounting field   User name*
         (installation) installation
         (dependent)   dependent
                          containing
                          account number
                          time est. etc.

(ii)   EXEC (execute) statements for informing the control program of the application program or procedure the user requires.

e.g.,   //STEP1   EXEC   OSIRIS
         stepname   *procedure name*

(iii)   DD (data definition) statements defining data files that are going to be needed by the user's program.

e.g.,   //DATAIN   DD UNIT=TAPE,VOL=SER=9999,DSNAME=MYDATA,
                        DISP=(OLD,PASS)
        ddname   Parameters defining location of
                        data--in this example a file
                        called MYDATA on tape number
                        9999 which already exists and
                        is to be 'passed' to a sub-
                        sequent step (DISP=(OLD,PASS)).*

All JCL statements have // (slash, slash) in column 1 and 2. The remainder of the card varies according to whether it is a JOB, EXEC or DD card. Details of OS/JCL syntax can be found in IBM reference manuals.

Except for the JCL, and the end of job signal (/*), setups designed to run under OS are almost exactly like those designed to run under MTS. The difference is that under OS the input and output assignments (e.g., for DICTIN and DATAIN) are done in the JCL rather than on OSIRIS commands. Shown below is a TABLES - MDC run.

```
//JOB1        JOB     (49999,3,,4),HEATH
// EXEC       OSIRIS
//DICTIN      DD DSNAME=MDICT,UNIT=TAPE,DISP=OLD,VOL=SER=99
//DATAIN      DD DSNAME=MYDATA,DISP=OLD,UNIT=TAPE,
//               VOL=SER=99,LABEL=2
//SCARDS      DD  *
&TABLES                    OSIRIS command
LABEL                      Program control cards for &TABLES
*
V=3-6
&MDC                       OSIRIS command
LABEL                      Program control cards for &MDC
V=10-19,6
&END                       OSIRIS command
/*                         End of job signal
```

OS setups for a number of jobs discussed in the text are shown below.

All computer installations have programs for copying cards to tape (or cards to disk, or data from tape to tape, or disk to disk). The example below uses the IBM utility program IEBGENER through a special procedure called COPY. You should inquire at your installation about your local utility program for copying.

H.1a SETUP: BATCH JOB TO
COPY CARDS TO TAPE
(USING A UTILITY PROGRAM)

```
//STEP 1      JOB     (468365,COPY),KLEM
//            EXEC    COPY
//DATAOUT     DD DSN=CUDATA,UNIT=TAPE,VOL=SER=9129,LABEL=1,
// DISP=(NEW,PASS),DCB=BLKSIZE=3520
//DATAIN      DD  *
  *
  *        Card data
  *
/*
```

The control cards given above will copy the card data to tape, creating what is known as a card image file. The DATAOUT DD card describes the file that is to be written. In this case a file with name CUDATA is being written to tape number 9129; the DCB parameter says that the records will be blocked --44 cards will be written in each block (BLKSIZE=3520). The DATAIN DD card describes the file that is being copied. In this case the file is on cards and the appropriate DD parameter is a single * which indicates that card data follows.

Another way to do the same job is to use the OSIRIS &COPYSORT command.

H.1b SETUP: BATCH JOB TO
COPY CARDS TO DISK
(USING &COPYSORT)

```
//A1          JOB     (468365,COPY),RATTENBURY
//            EXEC    OSIRIS
//COPYIN      DD  *
  *
```

```
        *                    Card data
        *
//COPYOUT      DD    DSN=CUDATA,DISP=(NEW,KEEP),UNIT=DISK,
//     VOLUME=SER=ISR001,SPACE=(TRK,(5),RLSE)
//SCARDS      DD    *
&COPYSORT
/*
```

In H.1b, just for an additional change from H.1a, the CUDATA dataset is
written to disk. The data file is new and is to be retained for subsequent
processing. ISR001 identifies the specific disk on which the file will
reside (inquire at your installation to find out the names of disks on
which you may write data files). The SPACE parameter specifies the amount
of space an disk that the file will need. It is wise to overestimate – the
ELSE keyword will cause the system to release unneeded space when the run
is finished.

H.2 SETUP: SORT CUDATA

```
//A1           JOB    (468365,SORT),PELLETIER
//             EXEC   OSIRIS
//SORTIN       DD DSN=CUDATA,UNIT=TAPE,VOL=SER=9129,DISP=OLD
//SORTOUT      DD DSN=CUSORTED,UNIT=TAPE,VOL=SER=9135,
//             DISP=(NEW,KEEP),DCB=BLKSIZE=3520
//SCARDS       DD       *
&COPYSORT      S=CH,A,7,2,CH,A,10,2,CH,A,5,2          REC=200
&END
/*
```

LABEL=1 is not necessary when data is on the first file of an input
tape; LABEL=1 is the OS default.

H.3 SETUP: MERCHECK THE
SORTED DATA

```
//A2           JOB    (468365,MERCH),WARREN
//             EXEC   OSIRIS
//DATAIN       DD DSN=SORTED,VOL=SER=9135,UNIT=T,DISP=OLD
//DATAOUT      DD     DSN=CUMERGED,VOL=SER=9138,
//   UNIT=T,DISP=(NEW,KEEP),LABEL=1
//SCARDS       DD    *
&MERCHECK
CHECKING MERGE OF CAMPUS UNREST DATA
PRINT=ALL MAXP=2 IDCOL=(7-8,10-11) MAXE=20 DUPK=1 CONS='400' CLOC=78
DECK=10 IDLOC=5   PAD='-
10II0II 0099000000000000000000000                                  40-
0'
DECK=12 IDLOC=5   PAD='-
   12II II                    999999  9999999              40-
0'
&END
/*
```

```
//A3        JOB      (468365,DICT),RATTENBURY
//          EXEC     OSIRIS
//DICTOUT   DD       DSN=CUDICT,UNIT=TAPE,VOL=SER=9129,
//          DISP=(NEW,KEEP),LABEL=2
//SCARDS    DD       *
&DICT
DICTIONARY FOR CAMPUS UNREST DATA
NREC=2 PRINT=(DI,OUTD)
V=1 NAME='STATE                Q1'   WID=2 COL=7 RECO=1
V=2 NAME='RESPONDENT ID        Q2'   WID=2 COL=10
V=3 NAME='NUMBER OF CALLS      Q22'  WID=1  COL=9 MD1=0
V=4 NAME='SEX                  Q23'  WID=1 COL=12 MD1=NONE
V=5 NAME='RACE                 Q24'  WID=1 MD1=0
V=6 NAME='MARITAL STATUS       Q4'   WID=1 MD1=0
V=7 NAME='AGE                  Q3'   WID=2 MD1=99
V=8 NAME='EDUCATION            Q5'   WID=1 MD1=0 TY=A
V=9 NAME='OCCUPATION           Q7'   WID=2 MD1=0 TY=C
V=10 NAME='EMPLOYMENT STATUS    Q6'   WID=1 MD1=0
V=11 NAME='FATHER S OCCUPATION  Q9'   WID=1 MD1=0 COL=22
V=12 NAME='HUSBAND S OCC        Q8'   WID=2 MD1=0
V=13 NAME='CHILDREN IN COLLEGE  Q12'  WID=1 MD1=0
V=14 NAME='WORK FOR POL PARTY   Q13'  WID=1 MD1=0
V=15 NAME='STUDENT VOICE        Q14'  WID=1 MD1=0
V=16 NAME='CONSPRIRACY          Q15'  WID=1 MD1=0
V=17 NAME='BAN SDS              Q16'  WID=1 MD1=0
V=18 NAME='VIET NAM             Q17'  WID=1 MD1=0
V=19 NAME='LOT OF AVERAGE MAN   Q18'  WID=1 MD1=0
V=20 NAME='CHILD INTO WORLD     Q19'  WID=1 MD1=0
V=21 NAME='COUNT ON PEOPLE      Q20'  WID=1 MD1=0
V=22 NAME='LIVE FOR TODAY       Q21'  WID=1 MD1=0
V=23 NAME='NEAREST LARGE CITY   Q25'  WID=20 TY=A COL=12  RECO=2
V=24 NAME='R S COMMUNITY SIZE   Q27'  WID=1 MD1=0 COL=21 RECO=1 TY=C
V=25 NAME='DIST FROM CITY       Q26'  WID=3 MD1=999 COL=32 RECO=2
V=26 NAME='TRAVEL TIME TO CITY  Q10'  WID=3 ND=1 MD1=99.9
V=27 NAME='NEW YORK TIMES       Q11'  WID=1 MD1=9 COL=40 ND=0
V=28 NAME='ANN ARBOR NEWS       Q11'  WID=1 MD1=9
V=29 NAME='DETROIT FREE PRESS   Q11'  WID=1 MD1=9
V=30 NAME='WALL STREET JOURNAL  Q11'  WID=1 MD1=9
V=31 NAME='CHRISTIAN SCIECE MON Q11'  WID=1 MD1=9
V=32 NAME='DAILY WORKER         Q11'  WID=1 MD1=9
V=33 NAME='WASHINGTON POST      Q11'  WID=1 MD1=9
&END
/*
```

H.5 SETUP: CORRECTING NON-
NUMERIC CHARACTERS IN
CAMPUS UNREST DATA--
THE &'s and -'S

```
//J4       JOB    (468365,TRAN),SMITH
//         EXEC   OSIRIS
//DICTIN   DD DSN=CUDICT,VOL=SER=9129,LABEL=2,UNIT=TAPE,DISP=OLD
//DATAIN   DD DSN=CUMERGED,VOL=SER=9138,UNIT=TAPE,DISP=OLD
//DICTOUT  DD DSN=CUDICT4,UNIT=TAPE,VOL=SER=9129,DISP=(NEW,PASS),
//               LABEL=2
```

```
//DATAOUT DD DSN=CUDATA4,UNIT=TAPE,VOL=SER=9129,DISP=(NEW,PASS),
//              LABEL=3
//SCARDS DD      *
&RECODE
 IF V8 EQ '0' THEN V8=0
 IF V8 EQ '1' THEN V8=1
 IF V8 EQ '2' THEN V8=2
 IF V8 EQ '3' THEN V8=3
 IF V8 EQ '4' THEN V8=4
 IF V8 EQ '5' THEN V8=5
 IF V8 EQ '6' THEN V8=6
 IF V8 EQ '7' THEN V8=7
 IF V8 EQ '8' THEN V8=8
 IF V8 EQ '9' THEN V8=9
 IF V8 EQ '&' THEN V8=10
 IF V8 EQ '-' THEN V8=11
&END
&TRANS
RECODE AMPS AND DASHES.   REFORMAT TO ONE LOGICAL RECORD PER CASE.
R=1 V=1-33
V=8 WID=2 TYPE=C
&END
/*
```

See also Appendix D, "Using OSIRIS IV on IBM machines without MTS," in
the OSIRIS IV Manual [10].

171

OSIRIS SYSTEM OVERVIEW, DATA STORAGE, HARDWARE REQUIRE-
MENTS, COMMANDS, AND DISTRIBUTION INFORMATION[17]

I.1 System Overview

OSIRIS.IV is the current version of a software package which has been
evolving for many years at the Institute for Social Research, The University of Michigan. It makes use of the latest practical knowledge to reduce
costs and provide increased capacity and flexibility in the areas of data
management and statistical analysis. OSIRIS.IV is designed to serve a
broad community of users and has facilities for handling data collected for
a wide range of purposes. In addition to the usual basic statistics and
functions, such as cross-tabulations and classical regression and correlation analysis, several special techniques are available for handling
nominal- and ordinal-scale data and for calculating sampling errors for
complex designs. OSIRIS.IV also has a full range of well integrated data
management facilities; of special interest are the ability to handle
weighted data, a powerful general purpose recoding facility, matrix input
and output, and hierarchical datasets with variable length records. Virtually any mode of data can be used directly in OSIRIS.IV for up to 32,000
permanent variables. Among its other capabilities are facilities for:

- Defining, modifying, and displaying variable attributes

- Copying and sorting data

- Checking data for "wild" or inconsistent code values

- Correcting data

- Displaying data

- Building and modifying rectangular or hierarchically structured data
  files

- Subsetting and transforming data

- Transforming data values, through arithmetic and logical operations
  both within and across records

- Aggregating records

- Converting, subsetting, and displaying matrices

- Generating univariate and bivariate frequency distributions and related statistics

- Generating scatter plots

- Correlation and multiple regression analysis

- Univariate and multivariate analysis of variance

---

[17]This material was taken from material prepared by the Survey Research
Center Computer Support Group (April 1984)

- Multivariate analysis using ordinal and nominal predictors

- Factor analysis

- Multidimensional scaling

- Cluster analysis

- Sampling error calculations

- Reading SAS, SPSS, OSIRIS.III and hierarchical datasets and free format data records

OSIRIS.IV is not a static system; resources are being invested in its improvement and extension, and updates or new releases will be issued as changes are made. Commands currently being developed or planned include commands for building and maintaining network data structures.

Standard and consistent parameter keywords make OSIRIS.IV easy to learn and use, and minimize the size and complexity of the required documentation. To use OSIRIS.IV, the user supplies the following items, as appropriate:

- OSIRIS.IV commands indicating which functions are desired

- Data formatted either as an OSIRIS.IV dataset or matrix

- Recode statements creating new variables or transforming existing ones

- Entry definitions indicating how groups of variables are to be assembled from a structured file

- Control statements specifying variables and parameters, optionally defining a subset of the data to be processed

OSIRIS.IV is an open system; it is relatively easy in most instances to read data which are stored in character or binary form directly into an OSIRIS.IV command. Another facet of the system's openness is the ability to take any OSIRIS.IV dataset and reformat it for use by other software. It is relatively easy to move outside the system; the data are not locked into OSIRIS.IV. Finally, the user may add programs which use OSIRIS.IV subroutines and hence use the common control statement language and OSIRIS.IV datasets. Thus the software may be augmented to meet the user's special needs.

In addition to the basic user manual "OSIRIS.IV: Statistical Analysis and Data Management Software System," there are many related publications of the Institute for Social Research that can serve as useful supplements.

I.2 Data Storage

Every OSIRIS.IV variable has a number and a fixed set of attributes associated with it, such as the location of the variable within each record of the data file, the variable width, type, number of decimal places and the values to be treated as missing-data. This information is stored in a dictionary file, one record per variable. Once this information is stored in the dictionary, it need not be respecified by the user--variables are referenced by their associated variable numbers. Dictionaries are easily created or revised with the &DICT command.

Data may be stored in a variety of modes including character numeric, binary, packed and zoned decimal, and alphabetic.

Note: <u>OSIRIS.III datasets are compatible with OSIRIS.IV</u>; OSIRIS.IV can both read and create datasets for use in OSIRIS.III.

OSIRIS.IV datasets have two possible configurations:

a. <u>rectangular</u>: all variables for one data case are stored in one record and each variable occupies the same relative location within each record:

	V1	V2	V3	V4	...
CASE 1					
2					
3					
4					
.					

b. <u>structured</u>: variables are collected into "groups" each with its own record length:

GROUP 1	V1	V2	V3	V4	V5	
GROUP 2	V6	V7	V8			
GROUP 3	V9	V10				
GROUP 4	V11	V12	V13	V14	V15	V16

Selected variables from different groups may be joined together to create a rectangular record for a given run.

The first step in the creation of an OSIRIS.IV rectangular dataset is to build an OSIRIS.IV dictionary file, usually via the &DICT command. Once the dictionary has been created the data may be read directly by OSIRIS.IV without any special "file building."

A structured dataset is built from individual rectangular files via the &SBUILD or &UPDATE command. This type of dataset is used where there is not only a relationship between variables within a rectangular dataset, but also a relationship, usually hierarchical, between the various

175

datasets. Each rectangular dataset becomes one or more groups in the structured dataset. A simple example is one rectangular dataset containing only household data and another containing additional data for individual members of each household combined by &SBUILD into a single structured dataset.

When a structured dataset is used in OSIRIS.IV, the user gives instructions via the &ENTRY command as to how the groups are to be arranged to create temporary rectangular records called "entries." This restructuring of the groups permits analysis to be performed on a wider range of entries than is possible with simple rectangular records and can thereby save numerous data management steps. The dictionary for the structured dataset may contain a default entry definition which is used to restructure the dataset when no other instructions are given via the &ENTRY command.

The advantage of a structured dataset is that for many data files, a more efficient storage mode is achieved in terms of space and cost of processing. This storage technique is more flexible and powerful than other data storage techniques, and permits larger datasets to be analyzed than in other systems.

I.3 Hardware Requirements

The hardware requirements for OSIRIS.IV are an IBM 360 or 370 computer, or an IBM-compatible machine such as an AMDAHL 470 V/6, with at least 150K bytes of main storage, the equivalent of 1000 to 3000 tracks, 7294 characters each, of disk work space, and sufficient peripheral devices for user input and output files. The computer must be operated under MTS, the OS/360 or MVS operating system, or equivalent.

I.4 Synopsis of Commands in OSIRIS.IV

Preparing Data for Input

&COPYSORT– Copies, reblocks and/or sorts OSIRIS.IV and non-OSIRIS.IV files.

&DICT   - Creates, corrects, modifies, or adds to existing dictionaries, and adds code category labels to a dictionary.

&FREE   - Creates an OSIRIS.IV dataset from an input dictionary and format-free data records.

&MATRIX   - Enters one or more matrices into OSIRIS.IV. Each matrix is assigned a unique number which is used to reference it in subsequent commands. Matrices created by OSIRIS.IV are entered following an &MATRIX command. Matrices created by other systems may be read by providing the appropriate control statements.

&SASFILE   - Creates an OSIRIS.IV dataset from a SAS internal file.

&SPSSFILE - Creates an OSIRIS.IV dataset from an SPSS internal file.

&MIDASFILE - Creates an OSIRIS.IV dataset from a MIDAS internal file, (for MTS systems only).

176

Checking and Correcting Datasets

&CONCHECK - Used with &RECODE, provides a consistency check capability
to test for illegal relationships between values for groups
of variables. &CONCHECK takes user specifications indicating data inconsistencies from tests made in &RECODE and
displays information identifying each inconsistency.
&RECODE and &TRANS or &FCOR can be used to correct the inconsistencies.

&FCOR - Provides file correction capabilities for rectangular and
structured OSIRIS datasets. It corrects values for any of
the variables in any data case, adds a completely new
record, or deletes an old one.

&MERCHECK - Detects and corrects merge errors for unit-record datasets
(e.g., cards) such as missing, duplicate, or invalid
records. The command produces a file in which each data
case has the same structure: A perfect merge of decks.

&WCC - Verifies whether a set of variables has only legitimate
data values and lists all invalid codes by case ID and
variable number. Once the bad code values have been identified, they may be corrected with &FCOR.

Displaying Datasets

&CBLIST - Displays OSIRIS.IV dictionary-codebooks.

&DSLIST - Prints a dictionary and/or a subset of variables from an
OSIRIS dataset. A variety of formats is available.

Building and Modifying Structured Datasets

&SBUILD - Builds an OSIRIS.IV structured dataset from one or more
rectangular datasets. The basic unit of a structured
dataset is a collection of related variables called a
"group." A group has the same characteristics as a rectangular dataset: All the records are the same length and each
variable is in the same relative location within each
record. However, a structured dataset may contain many
different groups, each with its own set of variables, and
some logical relationship which ties them together.

&ENTRY - With most structured files, the groups of variables created
by &SBUILD can be combined in several ways. Each distinct
combination of groups forms an entry, a single set of variables corresponding to a "case" in a rectangular file.
&ENTRY allows the user to define or redefine the entry to
be formed from the groups in the structured file, allowing
the user to specify how the structured file is to be rec-
tangularized.

&UPDATE - Builds or updates OSIRIS.IV rectangular or structured
datasets from one or more OSIRIS.IV rectangular or structured datasets. &UPDATE can add, delete, or replace cases

177

or variables in a rectangular dataset, and add, delete, or replace groups, records, or variables in a structured dataset.

&SENTRY - Builds an OSIRIS.IV structured dataset from a non-OSIRIS hierarchically structured data file and an &DICT description of the non-OSIRIS hierarchically structured file. &SENTRY can also input ID values where none exist in the data.

Transforming Datasets

&AGGREG - Aggregates individual records into group records defined by the user. Computes summary descriptive statistics.

&MATRANS - Changes the type of a matrix, prints a matrix, subsets a matrix, and changes variable numbers and names in a matrix.

&RECODE - A powerful recoding and variable transformation feature is available with almost all OSIRIS.IV analysis and data management commands. The &RECODE facility can create new variables from any arithmetic combination of existing variables; can bracket or recode variables according to specified tables; and has several special features such as creating "dummy variables" and combination variables. In addition, a modest amount of aggregation and disaggregation may be accomplished via &RECODE.

&TRANS - Creates a rectangular OSIRIS dataset from specified input variables. &TRANS can convert the mode of the variables, and can also change the dictionary type for compatibility with other systems. It also allows the subsetting of cases. Additionally, &TRANS can be used to insert new variables created or modified by &RECODE into the dataset, thereby making permanent copies of them.

Frequency Distributions and Associated Statistical Measures

&SCAT - Is a bivariate analysis command that produces scatter diagrams, univariate statistics, and bivariate statistics. The scatter diagrams are plotted on a rectangular coordinate system; for each combination of coordinate values that appears in the data, the frequency of its occurrence is displayed. &SCAT is particularly useful for displaying bivariate relationships if the numbers of different values for each variable are large and the number of data cases containing any one value is small.

&TABLES - Produces univariate or bivariate frequency tabulations and percentages, and univariate statistics by stratum. &TABLES may also be used to produce quantiles and several non-parametric measures of association and significance for ordinal or nominal data: the Mann-Whitney u, the Kruskal-Wallis h, gamma, Kendall's tau's (a, b and c), lambda, lambda a, lambda b, Leik-Gove's D for nominal data (corrected), chi-square, Cramer's V, G-square, Gini coefficient and Lorenz plot, Goodman and Kruskal's tau's (a and b) and Cohen's Kappa.

&USTATS   – Computes means, standard deviations, and minimum and maximum values for a given set of variables. Optionally, it will compute these statistics for each variable for each specified subset.

Correlation and Regression Analysis

&MDC   – Computes Pearson product-moment correlation coefficients for all pairs of variables in a list, or for all combinations of variables, one of which is from one list and another of which is from a second list or for selected pairs of variables. &MDC inputs missing-data using either a pair-wise or a case-wise algorithm.

&PARTIALS   – The n-th order partial-correlation coefficient (partial r) and the standardized partial regression coefficient (beta) are computed for each pair in a set of variables, holding all other variables constant. In addition, the multiple correlation coefficient (R) is computed for each variable using all the other variables as predictors.

&REGRESSN   – Computes standard or step-wise multiple regressions with or without a constant term. It accepts interval or categorical (dummy) predictors. With the step-wise option, predictors may be forced into the regression before the step process begins. Data may be weighted or unweighted and will be subject to case-wise missing-data deletion. &REGRESSN will produce &RECODE control statements for computing residuals, if requested.

Analysis of Variance

&ANOVA   – Performs one-way analysis of variance on one or more independent and dependent variable pairs. &ANOVA will produce &RECODE control statements for computing residuals, if requested.

&MANOVA   – Performs univariate and multivariate analyses of variance and covariance using a general linear hypothesis model. Up to twelve factors (independent variables) can be used. If more than one dependent variable is specified, both univariate and multivariate analyses are performed. &MANOVA performs an exact solution with either equal or unequal numbers of observations in the cells; the sums of squares attributable to the factors are partitioned hierarchically.

Multivariate Analysis Using Ordinal and Nominal Predictors

&DREG   – Provides a maximum likelihood regression capability for a dichotomous dependent variable using either a linear or logit model. &DREG may also be used to analyze multiway

179

contingency tables whenever one dimension can be thought of as a dichotomous dependent variable.

&MCA — A command for multiple regression with categorical predictors, &MCA examines the relationships between several categorical independent variables and a single interval scaled dependent variable, and determines the effects of each predictor before and after adjustment for its intercorrelations with other predictors in the analysis. See Andrews, et al., Multiple Classification Analysis, for a complete description of the method used. &MCA will produce &RECODE control statements for computing residuals, if requested.

&MNA — Performs multivariate analysis of nominal-scale dependent variables. While the MCA technique described above assumes interval measurement of the dependent variable, &MNA is designed to handle problems where the dependent variable is a nominal scale. The independent variables may be measured at any level, including nominal. The program uses a series of parallel, dummy variable regressions derived from each of the dependent variable codes, dichotomized to a 0-1 variable.

&SEARCH — Searches among a set of predictor variables for those predictors which maximally increase the researcher's ability to account for the variance or distribution of a dependent variable. The question, "what dichotomous split on which single predictor variable will give us a maximum improvement in our ability to predict values of the dependent variable?," embedded in an interactive scheme, is the basis for the algorithm used in this command. &SEARCH divides the sample, through a series of binary splits, into a mutually exclusive series of sub-groups. Every observation is a member of exactly one of these subgroups. They are chosen so that, at each step in the procedure, the split into the two new subgroups accounts for more of the variance or distribution (reduces the predictive error more) than a split into any other pair of subgroups. The predictor variables may be ordinally or nominally scaled. The dependent variable may be continuous or categorical. &SEARCH is an elaboration of the OSIRIS.III AID3 and THAID programs.

Factor Analysis and Multidimensional Scaling

&CAP — Performs analysis on a single spatial configuration. It has the capability of centering, normalizing, rotating, and translating dimensions. It will perform a varimax rotation and principal axis solution.

&COMPARE — Is based on Schönemann and Carroll's procedure for "fitting one matrix to another under choice of a central dilation and rigid motion." The technique rotates one configuration (the problem space) to the space of the other configuration (the target space) to achieve a least-squares fit. In seeking the best fit, the rotation is a "rigid motion," which maintains the orthogonality of the axes. A typical application is to compare the configurations produced by nonmetric scaling analysis and factor analysis from the same data.

&FACTAN — Provides a general factor analysis package that includes numerous options for the application of various factor analytic tools currently in use. Separate factor analyses may be performed on various subsets of variables in a single run.

&MINISSA — (Michigan Israel Netherlands Integrated Smallest Space Analysis) is a nonmetric multidimensional scaling command. The input to &MINISSA is a matrix of similarity or dissimilarity coefficients (e.g., Pearson's r): The output is a geometric representation of the matrix in m dimensions. &MINISSA constructs a configuration of points in space using information about the order relations among the coefficients. It is usually possible to satisfy the order relations of the coefficients in fewer dimensions than would be necessary to reproduce the metric information. &MINISSA is an adaptation of the MINISSA program developed by J.D. Lingoes of The University of Michigan and E.E. Roskam of the University of Nijmegen.

Cluster Analysis

&CLUSTER — Performs hierarchical cluster analysis. Starting with a symmetrical matrix of measures of similarities or dissimilarities, &CLUSTER successively partitions the dataset into a set of clusters. Clustering methods include the minimum and maximum methods, the central vectors and coefficient alpha method for similarities, and the centroid distance and mean square error methods for dissimilarities.

Sampling Error Analysis

&PSALMS — Using the Taylor series approximation method, &PSALMS computes estimates and sampling errors for ratio means and totals for stratified clustered sample designs. &PSALMS accesses both weighted and unweighted data, and does not assume a simple random sample was taken. &PSALMS will optionally calculate sampling errors for parameters on subclasses of dataset.

&REPERR — Computes estimates of regression statistics and their estimated sampling errors for data from clustered sample designs using repeated replication techniques. Replications are created using one of three methods: Balanced half-sample, jackknife, or user-specified replications.

I.5 Distribution Information

For further information about OSIRIS.IV, contact

OSIRIS IV Distribution
Computer Support Group
Survey Research Center
Institute for Social Research
The University of Michigan
Ann Arbor, Michigan   48106

The Survey Research Center Computer Support Group is located in Room 3110, ISR. The phone number is (313)764-4417.